I LOVE THE INTERNET, BUT I WANT MY PRIVACY, TOO!

Simple Steps
Anyone Can Take
to Enjoy the Net
Without Worry

CHRIS PETERSON

PRIMA PUBLISHING

To Rich and Mike

Library of Congress Cataloging-in-Publication Data

Peterson, Chris.
I love the Internet, but I want my privacy, too! / Chris Peterson.
p. cm.
Includes index.
ISBN 0-7615-1436-8
1. Internet (Computer network)—Security measures. 2. Computer security.
3. Privacy, Right of. I. Title.
TK5105.875.I57P473 1998
005.8—dc20 98-22383
CIP

98 99 00 01 02 BB 10 9 8 7 6 5 4 3 2 1
Printed in the United States of America

How to Order
Single copies may be ordered from Prima Publishing, P.O. Box 1260BK, Rocklin, CA 95677; telephone (916) 632-4400. Quantity discounts are also available. On your letterhead, include information concerning the intended use of the books and the number of books you wish to purchase.

Visit us online at www.primapublishing.com

CONTENTS

ACKNOWLEDGMENTS

I do love the Internet. The Net has indeed made researching this book a pleasure. The federal government does an excellent job of having information available on the World Wide Web. I could review Congressional hearings, read studies, and review meeting agendas from the comfort of my study. No one had to look for the information and promise to mail it to me—I could get it myself in the middle of a cold, wet night. The Web sites of privacy organizations, such as the Electronic Privacy Information Center, and company associations were a tremendous resource as well.

While the Internet was good for baseline information, many people talked with me and shared their insights on privacy technologies and issues. I appreciate the help of Catherine Allen, John Burke, John Byrne, Larry DeWitt, Steve Emmert, John Fanning, Beth Givens, Deirdre Mulligan, John Mozena, Brian O'Shaughnessy, Shelley Pasnik, Joe Reagle, John Sabo, and Jerry Sheehan. These experts from government, industry, and the nonprofit community took time from frantic schedules to work with me, and I am grateful.

Special words of appreciation go to Kristine Gentry, Nancy Moy, and Dorothea Gross. Kristine verified, updated, and defined the resource section and helped until the end. Nancy developed all my figures and tables, researched anything and everything I asked her to, and attended to the hundred of details necessary to finish the manuscript. Dorothea read countless drafts of the manuscript. Her helpful suggestions, creative ideas, and insightful comments did much to improve the end product. To each of you, many thanks.

I enjoyed working with everyone at Prima Publishing. Jamie Miller and her associates are a professional and dedicated group, and I consider myself very fortunate to be associated with this team and company.

Thank you all. It has been a wonderful experience.

INTRODUCTION

Tired but satisfied—a nice combination of feelings, you think, as you board the airplane for home. The conference and exhibition had gone well. But as happens with any intense activity, you are mentally and physically exhausted.

That is probably why you don't encourage conversation with your seatmate on the plane. He, too, was at the conference and seems eager to engage in discussion. You respond to his introduction with a friendly handshake and a few cursory responses to his questions. Then, purposefully opening your briefcase, you take out your largest report, open it, ready your highlighter for action, and fall asleep.

The announcement jars you. The plane will be landing at Denver's airport shortly. You quickly ready yourself. Your seatmate is changing planes here, too. As you pull up to the gate, he wishes you a safe and speedy trip and hopes he'll be able to talk with you again . . . soon.

Four hours later you're home. Everyone is in bed but you just aren't ready yet. You turn on your computer and check your e-mail. As you scroll through the messages, you notice the latest message is from an address you don't recognize. You move to the entry and double-click.

The message appears on the screen. The first line says he hopes he has reached the correct person. Using your full name, he asks if you are the one he sat next to while traveling to Denver today. After reminding you of your brief but enjoyable conversation just hours ago, he talks about how he'd like to continue the discussion you started. Fortunately, he will be coming to your city in a few weeks for business. He mentions that he will be staying at a hotel close to your home and would love to meet for lunch or dinner if you are free. He concludes by telling you how much he is looking forward to seeing you.

You pause. You move your eyes to the opening sentence. There is your full name, including your middle name—the middle name you relegated to an initial years ago. Scrolling down the message you see that he is correct; the hotel where he is staying is near your home. But how does he know?

How in the world did he find you? You don't know whether you are annoyed by his invasion of your privacy or intrigued by the technology that enabled him to find you. You'd like to know how he did it—and how to see to it that it doesn't happen again.

He did it through the technological advance called the Internet, a phenomenon that makes accessible to each of us a source of vast information—some of which will make life easier, more productive, and more amusing. But this sea of information also contains details—personal details—about you.

Many find this thought unsettling, even creepy; others do not. People's feelings about privacy range from having mild privacy needs in limited parts to fierce protectiveness over the details of their lives. This book was designed to respond to the full spectrum of privacy concerns. Those of you with few concerns will be intrigued with the changes in personal information-handling in the Electronic Age. You will learn the identity and activities of cybersnoops and Webpeepers and will reap the rewards of increased awareness.

Some have a few concerns about personal information. For example, you don't mind giving up personal information as long as there is an exchange. As long as you are obtaining a benefit, fine, you may think. But when flooded with inappropriate advertisements, even the most nonchalant become annoyed.

Still others have specific privacy concerns—"pulse points," if you will. A pulse point could be your personal financial or medical information. Concern about keeping such information private may even be limiting your use of the Internet. For you, awareness and good practices will be provided, covering your Internet usage at home, work, and play. From e-mailing your boss to overseeing the Web sites your children visit, knowing the rules and cautions will ease your mind. You probably want more information, information that will help you understand your technology choices (without all the jargon) for protecting your electronic privacy. You want to take action in some spheres by removing your name or "opting out" of databases. You also want to know what government and industry are doing to ease your worries.

Finally, some of you are users for whom privacy is a powerful and passionate issue. You demand not only a complete understanding of the latest findings and events, but seek ways to engage in decision making. Your goal is to become a privacy advocate, or at least a savvy practitioner. The comprehensive resource information, including privacy groups and points of contact in this book, will provide you with current information and groups that share your concerns. Figure 1 summarizes the range of privacy concerns Internet users have.

Regardless of which category you fall into, reflecting on privacy and the Internet helps all of us. The Internet and the Electronic Age to which it belongs can be a vibrant part of all our lives if it is designed to serve us well. Now, during this embryonic stage of development, is the time to decide what we are willing to accept and what we will demand.

Throughout this book the implications of privacy concerns will be illustrated and evaluated. Chapter 1 contrasts the world of just fifteen years ago to the Electronic Age we live in now. It notes the differences that computers, databases, and (most of all) the Internet have made in the way government and business conduct their work. Your privacy pulse points and concerns will be investigated too. This sets the stage for chapters 2 and 3, which define the players, their motivations, their approaches, and

Category	Trait	Interest
Nonchalant	No concrete concerns	Awareness
	Mild concrete concerns	Good practices
Pulse Point	Specific concrete concerns (finance, medical)	Awareness Good practices
	Control concerns	Technology choices Policy options
Passionate	Strong concrete concerns	Awareness
	Strong control concerns	Good practices Technology choices Policy options Active involvement

FIG. 1:

Range of Privacy Concerns

their methods for obtaining and using your personal information. Chapter 2 concentrates on the quiet companies and government agencies with large databases for sale—full of personal information. It explores the invisible database industry's tried and true techniques for collecting personal information. Chapter 3 looks at companies with Web sites and home pages on the Internet and explores a number of new and surreptitious technologies these Web sites have developed for the purpose of learning about you.

Chapters 4–7 will, in a practical way, discuss how your personal information is handled in this new world and in what areas you are vulnerable. Employer monitoring of your Web surfing, credit card and identity theft risks while you shop on the Internet, and your vulnerability in social situations on the Web are reviewed in chapter 4. Chapter 5 highlights your medical information and the number of people besides your doctor who look at your medical records and see your family secrets. Chapter 6 discusses the special risks to children on the Internet. Details in each of these chapters are likely to surprise, perhaps alarm you. Chapter 7 continues the focus on your children and discusses a variety of ways to keep them safe on the Web. Good practices—habits you can easily incorporate into your everyday life that will safeguard you and your information—will be articulated throughout these chapters.

Chapters 8–11 go beyond good practices to technology, corporate self-regulation, government action, and international models. Chapter 8 returns to the adult world and reports on privacy-enhancing technologies available today and those under development for the future. Technology is a viable weapon to protect privacy, but it must be user-friendly and support the goals we establish. Chapter 9 is centered on industry self-regulation efforts. Several industrial groups have proposed frameworks and systems to improve privacy. Many are new and untested, but demonstrate an encouraging recognition of a shared problem. Chapter 10 is a case study of very private information being handled responsibly on the Internet. But the responsible handling did not occur effortlessly and the unanticipated problems relating to the public's privacy concerns were challenging.

Chapter 11 examines the government's role in the Internet privacy issue. At times the government appears to be moving far too slowly. But, on closer examination, one can see that progress is being made and behind-the-scenes efforts may prove more successful than legislation. The chapter concludes by detailing a serious privacy problem brewing across the Atlantic Ocean in Europe; it explores the dimensions of this dilemma and notes the potential ramifications.

The book closes with an extensive and far-reaching list of resources that include associations monitoring Internet privacy issues in general and privacy advocacy groups. It also contains pulse-point organizations and information sources on specific Internet issues relating to children, consumer fraud, and medical concerns. Technology resources and help advisories are listed as well.

Most important, this book is not created to be passive. The issues are real and often are shown to you in a vivid way. Two techniques conceived to involve you in your own privacy protection and, in a way, to personalize the issue for you are the Personal Privacy Profiles and the information resources on privacy. The Personal Privacy Profiles consist of short exercises in the first three chapters. Each takes no longer than fifteen minutes to complete and is designed to portray the ease with which others can obtain facts about you and, of course, to help you determine what information about you is on the Internet. After developing a Personal Privacy Profile from the exercises in chapters 1, 2, and 3, you can check out the addresses of Web sites for advice, technologies, and reference on privacy provided in the remaining chapters. For example, when a technology to anonymously visit Web sites is discussed, the Web site designation is listed so the reader can try the technology. This enables you to continue the interactive experience but with the tools (information and technology) to protect your privacy.

By the conclusion of this book, you will know what information about you is on the Internet. You will have a new awareness of the Internet privacy issue and will be able to gauge your feelings about your personal information. You will be armed with tools in the form of good practices and technology to protect yourself when you feel protection is appropriate. But you will also be apprised of issues outside your immediate control—industry self-regulation and government policies. Industry and government want to hear your opinions and respond to you as a consumer and a citizen. Your voice will help shape the flourishing Internet society of which we will all want to be part.

1

CYBERSNOOPS, WEBPEEPERS, AND YOU

Chapter 1 provides you with a way of identifying the privacy issues pertinent to you and your family. It contrasts the electronic world of today with the model of information collection and access of fifteen years ago. It also introduces you to the concept of "Personal Privacy Profiles," brief exercises at the conclusion of the first three chapters that highlight how easy it is for others to invade your privacy.

The amazing Internet can permeate nearly every aspect of your life. It can allow you to effortlessly tap into vast reservoirs of information. You can review and buy the latest bestseller, or even scope out your next vacation destination, with a quick point and click. You can even look up the phone number of a cousin living thousands of miles away in seconds. The magic of the Internet and the World Wide Web is that information is unfettered and free for anyone with the simple skills to unearth it.

But has this electronic information revolution compromised something even more precious than information freedom—your privacy? This is a difficult question to answer because most of us don't even realize how much of our privacy we have already surrendered. Many of you suspect you have surrendered more information than you would like—and you are right.

This book is written for you. It delves into your thoughts, concerns, and questions about privacy in the electronic age. It understands that you may be a weekend Web browser or regular user just discovering that your privacy—from sensitive financial information to Social Security numbers to medical information—is under attack. You may be just starting or planning to start investigating this new and exciting world of cyberspace, but want to begin carefully and not compromise beliefs and rights you hold dear.

INTERNET PRIVACY IS EVERYONE'S BUSINESS

You are not alone in your concerns about your privacy. In a national survey commissioned by Privacy and American Business, a report and information service, and conducted by Louis Harris and Associates, men and women from all over the country, of all ages and education levels, raised their voices about issues such as:

- Distrust in institutions that handle their personal information online
- Confidentiality of e-mail communication—more so than other widely used forms of communication, including telephone, fax, and mail
- Monitoring of chat room discussions
- Tracking of visits to Web sites
- Privacy for and vulnerability of children on the Internet and a bevy of related issues

This national survey provides quantifiable data proving that privacy is a major concern that keeps many of us from embracing this new electronic medium. The Harris study echoes on a national level what other studies have indicated over the years.

The Graphic, Visualization, and Usability (GVU) Center at Georgia Institute of Technology has conducted at least eight World Wide Web

(WWW) user surveys over the last four years. The findings show that at one time censorship was the top issue facing users of the Internet, followed by privacy. In the GVU's 8th WWW User Survey, privacy moved into the first position, with more surveyed users saying they "strongly agree" to the need for action, specifically new laws.

YOUR PRIVACY CONCERNS ARE UNIQUE

Surveys of Internet users reveal that most of their concerns are shared in a quantifiable and generalizable manner. But privacy is a personal issue. Experts don't even agree on a definition. Consider, if you will, your concerns about privacy on the Internet. Privacy might mean simply drawing the line at how far others can intrude into your affairs without reason. These are a set of limits that protects you from the curiosity of those in the physical world or cyberspace—whether your neighbors, businesses, or the government. These are concrete concerns.

Concrete—a material used to build buildings, roads, and bridges—is abundant, strong, and solid. Concrete privacy concerns center on the building materials of your life. For example, financial information—how much you earn, how you spend your earnings, and your portfolio of savings and investments—are details of your life that are personal, perhaps intimate. You may also consider them private. So, too, are the details like credit card numbers. It is awful to have someone take your identity, abuse it, then leave you to deal with the aftermath. And what about those very sensitive parts of your history? That "D" in high school chemistry, or something more serious—a tough or abusive time in your life—do they deserve to be hidden from electronic eyes?

To further define concrete privacy concerns, review the critical information about yourself and your family. This includes your political beliefs, financial investments, academic history, personal problems, and even your use of private time. Which pieces of information do you consider "very sensitive," information to which you limit access? When you give others access to such information, you do so because they have a compelling reason to know or you have an equally compelling reason to tell them. Notice, *you* are making the decision.

Then there is information that is merely "sensitive." You wouldn't want such details to appear in your local newspaper, but are less troubled by the effects of more people knowing sensitive than *very* sensitive information. Finally there is the multitude of facts that are commonly known about each of us.

Spend a minute thinking about what privacy means to you. Privacy is an issue that requires translation; it means different things to different people. Further, some people need more privacy than others do.

YOUR PRIVACY CHECKLIST

The Privacy Checklist in figure 1.1 will provide you with a snapshot of your own privacy issues and their rating or sensitivity in your life.

Look over your answers to the checklist. You may have identified several areas that let you know where you want to draw the line for "Webpeepers." This set of categories and ratings was presented to 25 people to elaborate on the concept of differing levels of sensitivity. This is not the quantitative undertaking of the GVU Center or Louis Harris and Dr. Westin; instead, it is a qualitative or illustrative exercise. The respondents included 12 men and 13 women with ages spanning the early-20s to mid-70s.

Two people refused to participate in the survey. Their reason: The questions were an invasion of their privacy! Another respondent did not consider any of the topics private areas. Of the others, the financial topic ranked the highest as "very sensitive," closely followed by medical/health, then by personal history. When combining both "very sensitive" and "sensitive" concern ratings, both the medical/health and the personal history categories overshadowed financial issues.

This soft look at concrete concerns shows the possible areas and degrees of sentiment and feeling. Note how the Internet intensifies these concerns. Intuitively, people understand the power of technology even if they do not thoroughly understand the technology itself. The power to obtain, process, and distribute information in the blinking of an eye in-

For each topic listed, check whether that topic for you is very sensitive to a need for privacy, sensitive (you won't want the whole world to know), or you are not concerned about who knows.

Topic	*Very Sensitive*	*Sensitive*	*Not Concerned*
Salary			
Financial			
Family members under 18 years old			
Medical/Health			
Personal History			
Voting Record			
Religious Beliefs			
Other—please list			

FIG. 1.1: Your Privacy Checklist

herently creates a concentrated emotional response when one is directed toward privacy invasion. This intensification will result in vehement responses to privacy threats. You will find examples in this book and probably in your own experience as well.

Gathering personal data about an individual has always been possible. But it was an activity only for the most determined before the electronic information explosion. Making a trip to a state or county government office could yield a cornucopia of information—but only after waiting in long lines, filling out endless request forms, and wading through cumbersome record books. In a recent trip to the courthouse, Rich P. was checking the property line between his home and his neighbor's. During his search he found his mortgage on file with his Social Security number, spouse's Social Security number, and even his wife's maiden name. All this data was in the piles of microfiche for anyone willing to drive to the courthouse and search. But getting personal data is getting increasingly easy. In today's world, we merely turn on (boot up) our computer and log onto the Internet. The information is readily available.

You may be like one survey respondent who does not have any "sensitive" topics. You may be one who has "nothing to hide." While you may have no concrete concerns, you certainly may have control concerns. Dr. Alan Westin, a privacy pioneer, offers this definition of the term.

> Privacy: the desire of people to choose freely under what circumstances and to what extent they expose themselves to others.

Think of control in terms of a driver in an automobile. The driver determines a route, speed, and maybe even decides to turn on the radio. The driver *controls* the vehicle. The car cannot, of its own accord, travel to places you have never been and don't want to go. A control concern then focuses on control of your personal information. As a driver makes decisions, so should you. If you decide to provide information to the Division of Motor Vehicles to obtain your driver's license, you are controlling where your information goes and how it is used. But if the DMV sells your information to others for purposes quite different, you have lost control of your personal information. Control of personal information includes deciding who has access to it, how others can use it, and what its value is to them.

THE INTERNET AND YOU

The value of your personal information has increased greatly over the past two decades. Its value is in the marketplace or, for our purposes, the "marketspace." In 1994, many thought only a million users would ever be part of the Internet. Two years later tens of millions used the Internet and the numbers are still growing (see table 1.1). In fact, every two seconds there is a new Internet user. The mounting flock is not your average public. These users attracted to the Internet are smart, educated, and affluent.

Internet users are participating in one of the most dynamic communities on the planet. It's a place full of fascinating people, innovative businesses, and interesting ideas. The Internet has enriched the lives of many. Table 1.2 provides a sample of what adult Internet users are doing.

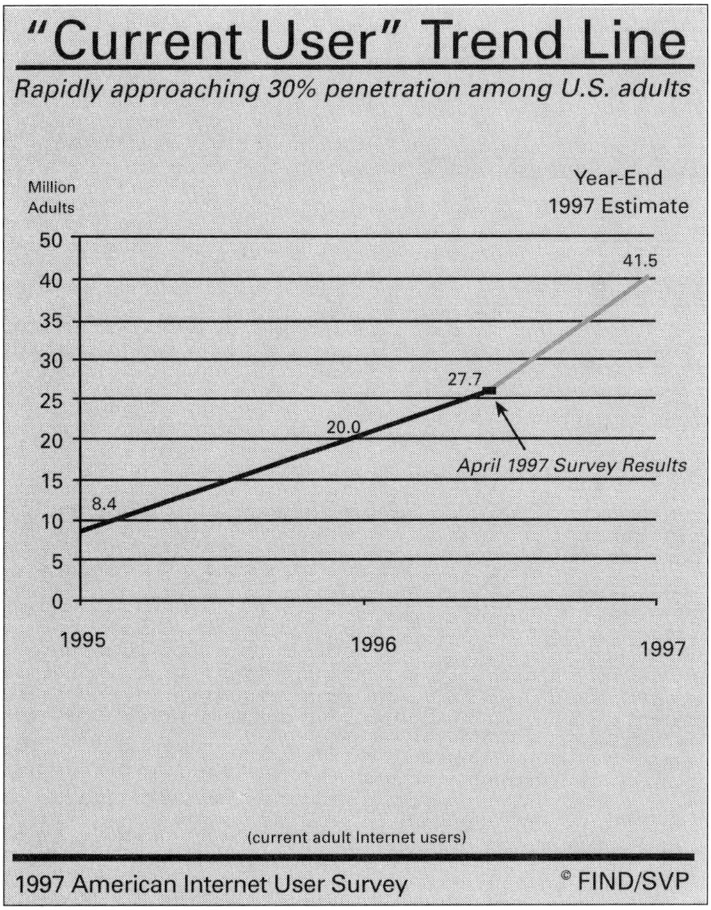

TABLE 1.1:

"Current User" Trend Line

Source: Cyberdialogue/FIND SVP, http://www.cyberdialogue.com

The characteristics of these current and potential users and the variety of information they are seeking make them attractive targets to businesses and corporations. And corporate cybersnoops have inquiring minds—especially now.

THE CUSTOMER-CONTROLLED MARKETSPACE

When the industrial revolution began and mass production was new, the marketplace was product-driven. Henry Ford could not have said it better

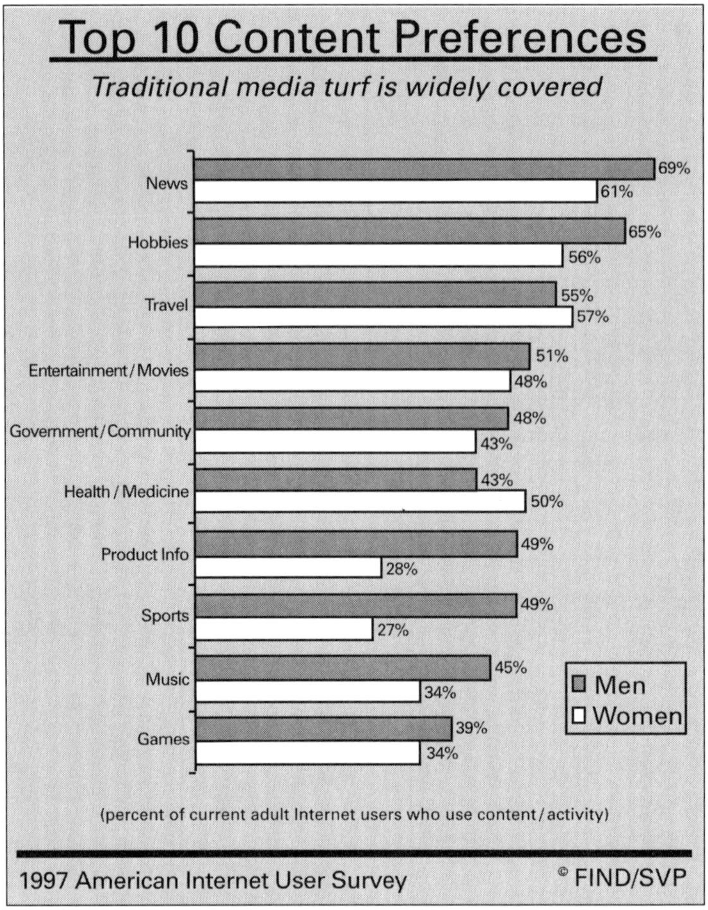

TABLE 1.2:

Top 10 Internet Content Preferences

Source: American Internet User Survey, 1997. New York: Cyberdialogue/FIND SVP, http://www.cyberdialogue.com

than when he described customer choices for the Model T: "You can have any color you want as long as it is black." Products were defined by manufacturers and a ready supply of consumers was prepared to buy.

But times change. Now the world of commerce is not product-driven, but is customer-controlled. Companies eagerly tailor their products to requirements of consumers like you and introduce new products to meet your specific needs. They want a one-to-one relationship with you; and to do this, they believe they need to know a lot about you.

So information about the customer—you—is gathered in amounts and ways Mr. Ford could never envision. Your personal data is gathered aggressively by companies striving to develop and sell products you may want. Collecting your vital statistics, merging it with other pieces of information about you, and making decisions based on it takes place at a feverish pace—without your knowledge. All these activities—collecting, merging, and exchanging—have value to the companies engaged in these efforts. Yet you are out of the picture. Your permission is not asked, and you are not reimbursed.

Think about the business articles you have read recently about new and improved products. Usually at least one sentence talks about the "target" customer or consumer. The product was developed to meet the requirements or desires of this target customer often called microtargetting. Now create a picture of the "target." Is your image a bull's eye affixed to each of us being stared at through the site of a rifle? Holding the rifle is the business. This is not a pleasant analogy, but may be accurate if consumer information is gathered actively without the consumer's knowledge and consent, then sold and resold to third parties. Even when you become aware of these actions because of their repercussions, you are denied access. These are control concerns at their most serious.

Although the idea of one-to-one relationships between companies and customers is laudable, it needs to be pursued with customers as *partners* with, not *targets* of companies. One way to encourage such partnerships is for consumers to have control over their information and to offer it willingly in circumstances they find acceptable. Now trust has been introduced. Trust is an excellent foundation for a relationship with companies and the Internet.

OTHER WEBPEEPERS

When people worried about their privacy two decades ago, the threat was not from the private sector. The government or "Big Brother" was the focus of worry. This worry was translated into laws in the 1970s and 1980s, laws which reined in the power of data gatherers at the federal level and made sure citizens could see the information the government had about them. States and local governments did not fall under this legislation and, as time passed, two trends accelerated. The first was the trend toward reducing taxes and the consequence of reducing services. This started many governments creatively exploring new streams of revenue. Private companies were eager to have the data state and local governments had and were willing to pay for it. An example of this is the sale of the Division of Motor Vehicle information. States and localities sold all or parts of information from citizens registering for a driver's license. This practice has been restricted.

Coupled with seeking new revenue sources to fund government services was a move to make information more available to residents. One way to do this was to put the information on a private network or the Internet. It did indeed make the information more available—to *everyone.*

Beyond the public and private sector, the individual cybersnoop lurks. It may be your neighbor, your boss, or your roommate looking for details. A mother may want to check out her daughter's new boyfriend. Or, your uncle may want to finally track down that fellow who owes him $20. The Internet makes it possible. The following Personal Privacy Profile exercise will prove it to you.

PERSONAL PRIVACY PROFILE NO. 1

To begin your first *Personal Privacy Profile,* you will want to gather some baseline information. The first exercise will show how easy it is for anyone in the country, or the world, to find out your phone number, address, and even a map to your home.

The World Wide Web (WWW), part of the Internet, will be the source of the sites you'll want to reach. The WWW is a relatively new phenomenon; however, the Internet has been around for a long time and was initially used by government and academic scientists. Quite frankly, the average person would not have found the Internet of 1975 very interesting. Then someone (Tim Berners-Lee) figured out a way to move easily from one computer file to another.

These computer files, called Web pages or home pages, are your destination. You will require access to a Web browser. The browser acts like a remote-controlled car in cyberspace; it is one of the ways you move from place to place. Two of the most common browers are Netscape Navigator and Microsoft's Internet Explorer.

You'll tell the browser where to go initially by typing in an address on the top line of your screen. When you arrive at the site, you'll be offered other choices that will move you to different locations. Now instead of using your browser to move from one place to another, you will use hyperlinks. Hyperlinks are easy to spot on a Web page. They will either be a word or a set of words in a different color, or a picture or graphic. When you move the mouse on top of the colored words or graphic, the mouse cursor line will turn into an index finger pointing. To make your choice, you will point your cursor to your selection then press your mouse twice. This system of pointing on hyperlinks and clicking will allow you to move around the home page/Web page and even to move from one home page/Web page to another.

If you don't have Internet access at work or home, ask a friend who does to help you. If you have access but have never done anything on the Web, have a teenager or knowledgeable adult standing by to help out.

A caution for those using the Internet for the first time. Web sites are occasionally down or not functioning. If this happens when you try to use Infoseek, here are some other Web sites you can try: www.switchboard.com, www.bigfoot.com, www.whowhere.com, and www.mapquest.com. The other possibility is that Web operators are constantly improving their Web sites so Infoseek may look different than described here. You should still be able to work your way through the site; it will just take slightly more time.

For your phone number/address, we will visit just one Web site. First, you will have to log into your Internet service provider, such as America Online or Prodigy. Or, it could be a local company that provides limited service and direct access to the Internet. (In northern Virginia, Erols is a popular choice.) You will connect to the Internet from these services. Internet will be a choice in one of the first few screens you see. Once you are connected, move the cursor to the top line. You will see the word "Location" or "Go To" followed by white space. If something is already written in the white space, erase it. Then type in the first address: http://www.infoseek.com. Once you are connected with the Infoseek home page, you will see a list of choices at the top of the page. The choices will be stock, news, maps, People&Business, reference, and yellow pages. Put your mouse on People&Business and double-click.

You have moved to the People&Business part of the Infoseek home page. You will now be asked to select "Find people" or "Find a business." Select "Find people" by clicking on the phone number and address circle. Then fill out the boxes with your first name, last name, and state. This may be all the system needs to find you. In seconds, a name or several names will appear with zip codes. Select the one that is you and click on the details box.

In the blink of an eye, your complete address and phone number will appear. This will only work if you have a listed phone number. If you are unlisted, most directories will not include you. Now, are you ready to get directions to your house? Go to the toolbar under edit to a box labeled "Back." Hit "Back" twice so you return to the beginning screen on the home page. Instead of clicking on "People&Business," you are going to click on "Maps."

The "Maps" screen will open, showing your choices of information. Select "Driving directions." You will be asked to input starting point and destination. Try your office to home or similar destination. You will be asked to select text-only directions or directions with map. Select the directions with map and enter. This may take nearly five minutes—a bit longer than obtaining your phone number and address, but lightning fast compared to getting directions in the physical world. So in less than ten minutes, even for a first-time Web search, you have readily found information about yourself. Imagine finding the same information without the help of the Internet. Even if you had the information at your fingertips, you would have taken many times longer and might not have such complete directions.

Dorothea G. found this to be true. She tried this for the first time using her name. The Internet quickly provided the requested address and phone number. Astounded, she wanted to test the system further. She then entered the name of her nephew—someone no one in her family had seen in years. He had simply disappeared. She guessed he might be living in Massachusetts but did not know the city or town. In less than a minute, the mystery was solved. His address and phone number showed up on the screen.

This exercise only looked at your address, phone number, and directions to your house. What about your life history? Companies collect, merge, and sell over the Internet all kinds of facts about you. These reference services or "look-up" companies know a great deal about you. Who are they telling?

2

THE DATA MONGERS AND YOU

This chapter examines the information industry. It will analyze the three main contributors of this industry: government, direct marketers, and professional reference services. You will become aware of the databases each contributor has, the kinds of personal information the databases contain, and the control (if any) you have over your information. The Personal Privacy Profile exercise will illustrate how information is collected in a public database then sold to a private vendor. The exercise will scan state and local records for bankruptcies and liens in your name.

THE TIMES THEY ARE A' CHANGING

Smalltown, USA—remember it? Once upon a time, that was where most Americans were born, grew up, worked, married, and died. Your neighbors knew your family history and just about everything about you. Your personal privacy was limited because of the familiar nature of small-town life. But at least you knew the people and had a good idea what they knew about you.

Population growth and the technology explosion have changed all this. With nearly 270 million people living in America, keeping track of all of them has become big business. Now you probably don't know the people or the companies that have access to your personal information. In fact, there are probably 25 to 100 databases on you—maybe more. And these databases are being sold and merged with other databases all the time.

With the ability to store massive amounts of information, transmit it electronically, and combine it with other information, our personal privacy is now the property of governments and corporations, not just the gossipy widow down the street.

Government, direct marketers, and professional reference services want to record information about everyone participating in our society. The direct marketers and reference services recognize that the information on individuals, from their ages to favorite flavor of ice cream, is valuable—how valuable depends on how descriptive it is. The more descriptive the information, the more uses it has. A person's Social Security number, for example, is of interest to a credit card company that wishes to verify the person's identity. A direct marketer would use this same piece of information to ensure that only one solicitation was sent to this person. But when this information is combined with other pieces of information—personal characteristics, interests, and buying habits—the value increases. Frequently the information is gathered for one purpose, then sold and used for another. The government—whether federal, state, or local—is a good example of an entity that does this.

BIG BROTHER IS WATCHING YOU

All levels of government collect vast amounts of information about individuals and businesses. They do so with our knowledge and our cooperation. We are aware of the information we provide when we complete our tax forms, when we register our cars, and when we move through the major life events such as marriage and parenthood. Public records of

Government Source	*Types of Personal Information*
Division of Motor Vehicles	address, date of birth, driver history, Social Security number, physical characteristics, type of automobile driven, accident reports
Property Records	name and address of owners, characteristics of house (square feet, number of rooms), mortgage holder and amount, appraised value, who sold the house and when
Voter Registration Records	address, party affiliation, last election you voted
Marriage/Divorce Records	maiden name of bride, dates of marriage/divorce, whether there were previous marriages
Civil and Criminal Court Cases	plaintiff and defendant names, lawyers' names, case file numbers, arrest records

FIG. 2.1:

Public Record Databases

Source: Nora Paul of the Poynter Institute of Media Studies, http://www.hvu.nl/~pverweij/nora/carpeopl.htm

these activities are generally available to anyone and, at a minimum, contain our names, addresses, and spouse's names. They often provide much more. Race, gender, date of birth, marriage, divorce, professional licenses, bankruptcy, and asset holdings are available as well. Figure 2.1 points out many of the information sources, what they contain, and even what information you need in order to search the databases.

Over the past few years, many state and local government agencies have been moving toward electronic access to their records. Electronic access brings all the information together in one place—cyberspace. Previously, you had to go to the state registrar's office to find someone's date of birth and birthplace, the county clerk's office to find a person's date of marriage and spouse's name, and the county recorder's office to find out real property ownership. As more states and county governments computerize, this information and more will be widely available from the Internet—available at any time from the comfort of home or work.

Many states already have computerized systems on electronic networks ready to be accessed. For example, the Kansas State Legislature in 1990 created INK. This system (http://www.ink.org/ink-index.cgi) has a modest annual subscription fee and contains a wide variety of public records. You can search for motor vehicle and driver records, corporation status, district court records, medical boards, vital records, and much more.

Indiana has placed a limited number of public records and registries on the Internet. Locating state records on abandoned property, land, driver's licenses, vehicle liens, titles, and registrations are as simple as typing in http://www.state.in.us. This makes information easily available to the citizens of Indiana—and anyone else. It provides other services, too. A "Sex Offender Registry" comprises information from several sources, chief among them the Indiana Criminal Justice Institute. You can search this registry checking for those convicted of:

- Rape
- Criminal deviant conduct
- Child molestation
- Child exploitation
- Vicarious sexual gratification
- Child solicitation
- Child seduction
- Sexual misconduct with a minor
- Incest

What a help this service is to employers concerned about hiring a person convicted of a sex offense against a child—and to the community and its nonprofit organizations looking for youth league coaches and scout masters. Many of the searches in Indiana are free or with a nominal charge.

DATABASE ERRORS

One concern with any major database—whether government or commercial—is accuracy. The journalist who checked on his marriage records and found that he was listed as the bride is the victim of one form of inaccuracy.[1] Although his is a good story to tell at parties, it is not life threatening. A dated but dramatic illustration of the impact errors in databases have on innocent people is the Sklar case. Richard Lawrence Sklar was returning home to Southern California from a Christmas holiday in England. U.S. Customs officials at Los Angeles International Airport ran a routine check on the passengers of the TWA flight and found that Sklar was wanted for his part in an Arizona real-estate scam. Over the next two days, the 58-year-old passenger was strip-searched, moved from one holding cell to another, and handcuffed to several violent offenders. There was one problem: Customs agents had the wrong man. The gentleman they were holding was a professor of political science at the University of California, Los Angeles. This wasn't the first time he had been mistaken for the real-estate scam artist. He had been fingerprinted on three separate occasions over 12 years.[2]

Vickie Denise Johnson, a resident of the Washington, D.C., area, suffered the tribulations of database errors twice. In 1985 she was taken into custody when she was picking up a birthday cake for her son's sixth birthday. Her sister had used Vickie's name when she was on the run from a burglary and assault charge. Police unknowingly arrested Vickie instead of Randi, and she spent one day and night in jail until the problem was thought to be resolved. But Vickie had trouble with employers over the next decade because her name wasn't cleared entirely from the criminal database.[3]

Even more confusing was when her name appeared in a Baltimore County computer in connection with child abuse. Vickie had never lived or worked in Baltimore County. But because her name appeared on this list, she was fired in 1996 from her position as child-care director of a YMCA center. This situation, too, was found to be a data error. In all, Johnson lost three jobs and spent years trying to rectify these database errors.

Errors such as these can certainly have harmful repercussions. In these cases, the mistakes occur in public information in government databases. The victims know who to talk to about correcting the errors, even if it takes years. But what happens when a government sells information that was voluntarily provided by the individual for an express purpose? When such information is sold, it will be used in a totally different manner, for purposes the individual was not aware of when he or she first provided it.

Opting Out of a Database

A driver's license contains a tremendous amount of personal information. It usually has name, address, height, weight, gender, eye color, date of birth, and visual impairments. In over half the states, a driver's license can also list the individual's Social Security number. Many states, to raise revenue from new sources, began selling part or all the information on these databases to commercial organizations for marketing and reference purposes. Many individuals found this very upsetting. The uproar these people created resulted in the Driver's Privacy Protection Act of 1994, which went into effect in September 1997. Although its validity is under dispute in the courts, the law will provide individuals with ways to control their driver license information through the use of "opt-outs." Opting out is when an individual suppresses his or her name in the database. However, this situation only pertains to drivers' licenses; it is not universally applicable.

For example, an individual provides the county recorder of deeds with information about the purchase price of a home and the identity of any lien holders in order to have the title recorded. The county may then sell this information, or provide it free, to members of the public, including direct marketers and reference services. A direct marketer might merge the information from county recorders with other information, such as a list of subscribers to a home-furnishing magazine, to develop a targeted mailing list for household-related products and services. A reference service might take the same information from the county recorders and sell it as part of a broader database that can be searched by the person's name or address.[4]

A final thought before moving away from government databases: Government records in our democratic society are open to the public to ensure a free flow of information. Many individuals, especially those passionate about their privacy, may consider certain aspects of public records private. Even those not passionate about privacy may be concerned about social forgiveness. Is there a time when a person has a fresh start? Not if their records are available.

COMMERCIAL CYBERSNOOPS

Over three-quarters of commercial companies in America use direct marketing to inform others about their products and services. But corporate America is not the only group using this mechanism. Nonprofits, education associations, political groups, and other organizations raise money, recruit new members, and alert people to important issues via direct marketing. Usually, the outreach method for direct marketing is telephone or mail. E-mail is slowly emerging as a direct marketing technique; it will be discussed further in chapter 3.

Which Lists Are You On?

Direct marketers rely on lists designed to target individuals likely to respond. If you buy outdoor equipment from athletic catalogues, you are a likely customer for their clothing catalogue or their credit card. The information comes from consumer surveys, warranty or response cards, and customer purchases over the telephone. This information may be merged with other lists. Two common possibilities for merging are public records and magazine subscriptions.

A list broker handles many lists. A company considering launching a direct marketing campaign will contact the list broker and rent one of the lists. The company does not actually physically receive the list. Rather, the broker arranges for the mailings to the list names as part of his or her service. The list is rented for a limited number of uses and for a specific identified solicitation. Prices range from $35 to $250 per thousand names. Catalogue sales benefit greatly from direct marketing.

The catalogue business is conducted on such a large scale that even small gains in the percentage of people who respond to a catalogue can translate into hundreds of thousands of orders. To get those small gains, catalogues use mailing lists to determine who the most receptive customers are. One major rule for preparing such lists has emerged: The best catalogue buyers are previous catalogue buyers. So, catalogue companies rent each other's mailing lists to find new customers.

Direct marketing certainly interrupts our dinner hour with phone calls and fills our mailboxes. But in some cases, it may be welcome. If you buy running shoes from a specialty shop in San Diego, you may enjoy being on a list that would bring to your attention other running-related products. On the other hand, if inappropriate contacts happen, you will want to remove your name from the list. To do so, contact:

Direct Marketing Association
Mail Preference Service, Box 9008
Farmingdale, NY 11735

DMA will put you in its computerized file and send it to the estimated 3,600 subscribing organizations to remove you from its lists. There is no comparable method for e-mail solicitations, as you'll see in the next chapter.

THE LOOK-UPS

Look-ups are also known as reference services, the dial-up information industry, locators, and individual reference services. They gather in one place a plethora of facts about you. Although most only sell their information to other commercial or professional companies, several look-up services are available directly to individuals. If you are working in a company with access to one of these databases, you could sit at your computer with only a person's name and address and develop a detailed profile. You could discover the person's prior addresses, date of birth, and telephone number (even if the number is unlisted). With slightly more effort and maybe more money, you can learn the person's occupation, Social Security number, and financial commitments, including the value of his or her house and the property taxes paid on it. In some cases, you can find the names of the person's neighbors and what they think about him or her. The information comes from public records, public sources like newspaper reports, and from other information providers. You can do this for others, and others can do it to you.

The Growing Hunger for Information

The demand for look-up services and the information they accumulate is expanding. The growth stems from two factors, one of which is the increase in population and mobility. There are simply more people, and organizations need to be able to tell them apart. In 1900, the resident population in the United States was 76,212,168. In 1990, the resident population had grown to 248,709,873. A new person is added to the U.S. population every 15 seconds. And the population is more mobile than ever before.

When Smalltown, USA was mentioned at the beginning of this chapter, the context suggested was that of being in one place for an entire lifetime. That is certainly not the case today. The mobility of Americans has dramatically increased. In 1996 alone, 42,537 people moved. This occurs every year and confounds the task of identifying people.

Companies need to know that the Robert Jones to whom they want to give a loan is the correct Robert Jones. This presents a specific problem that is a natural outcome of increased population—common names. One database contained 76,000 Robert Jones! These services help determine who is who. So we have more people, more common names, and more moving about, and none of these trends will diminish.

The second factor is the application and expectation of these services. When you bought a car 15 years ago, waiting five days for approval of your car loan was normal. This would not be acceptable today. Approval is expected on the spot. Whether for credit approval, employment verification, legal statutes, or government benefit purposes, all service-offering entities need to use reference services. And they need them to be easy to use and fast.

Credit Bureaus—Where the Power Begins

Reference services are playing a significant role in business and government. But, this is not a homogenous group. In fact, a number of credit-reporting companies do business in this country. Three of the largest and most recognized are: Equifax in Atlanta, Georgia; Experian (formerly TRW Information Systems and Services) in Orange, California; and Trans Union in Chicago, Illinois. These systems not only manage their own data; they provide data processing services for over 400 local independently owned automated credit bureaus. Consumer reporting agencies or credit bureaus know seemingly everything about your financial life. They gather information from identifying information (name and previous used names, current and past address, birth date, and Social Security number), credit information, public record information, and inquiries. Credit information is sold to the agencies from banks, finance companies, merchants, credit card companies, and other creditors. The information they sell usually is focused on the type of credit extended, the amount and terms of the credit, and the payment history.

Only information that comes from this group can be used to approve or decline a loan or refuse employment. And credit bureaus provide all the information necessary to make this decision. Accounts with banks, retailers, credit card issuers, and other lenders are recorded. The report lists accounts by type, opening date, credit limit and current debt, payment histories, and other information.

The FCRA to the Rescue

Credit bureaus or consumer reporting agencies have tremendous power. The power comes from an in-depth knowledge of your financial life. Because personal financial information is such a sensitive topic, this group of reference services is regulated by the federal government. To protect your privacy, these agencies' operations are governed by the Fair Credit Reporting Act (FCRA). The FCRA ensures appropriate information use in a number of ways. Consumer reporting agencies are prohibited from disclosing these consumer reports to anyone who does not have a legitimate purpose to see them. If you are denied credit or employment based on these reports, you must be notified. After notification you have the right to review your record. Finally, a procedure by which you can correct inaccurate information is in place.

While consumer reports cannot be sold to those without a clear credit intention, "credit header information" can be. Header information is name, current and previous address, any alias, date of birth, and Social Security number. Unlike the financial information in the consumer report, this header information is deemed less sensitive and does not come under FCRA regulation.

When the consumer reporting agencies sell header information, they usually sell it to other reference services. These reference services—such as Lexis-Nexis, CDB, and DBT—will merge information to form their own databases. Public records will join credit header information to provide more detailed information about a person. These groups of reference services are called professional reference services and they sell to commercial and professional companies.

Information for Sale–Professional Reference Services

Professional Reference Services are so named because they do not deal with individuals. Their clients are law firms; private investigators; federal, state, and local governments; and federal law enforcement agencies (including the Secret Service)—just to name a few. There are no federal laws restricting the operation of these companies. And they have a wide spectrum of business practices. Some of their responsible business practices are:

- Monitoring usage to detect any significant changes
- Conducting background checks on users
- Restricting access or intended use of information

But not all professional reference services adhere to good practices and no one knows when they stray or when to take corrective action. This is an industry that is unregulated with little oversight and little accountability. What's more, the industry is virtually invisible to most Americans—even though they hold an enormous amount of sensitive information.

Beth Givens, project director of Privacy Rights Clearinghouse, confirmed this in her testimony before the Federal Trade Commission (FTC) in 1997. Her comments were based on thousands of consumer complaints over the past five years. At this hearing she described the plight of Bronte Kelly, who had been a clerk in a department store. Unfortunately, he had been out of work for several years. Sure, he had been invited to many interviews, but was puzzled that he never was offered a position. Finally, in frustration, he urged the human resources manager in one of the interview sites to tell him where things were going wrong. The response was that the database they used to prescreen job candidates had Kelly listed as a shoplifter. Naturally, no retail department store would hire a shoplifter.

But Kelly wasn't a shoplifter. His wallet had been stolen and the thief who stole the wallet went on to commit this crime in one of the department stores. With Kelly's identification on him, the store attributed the crime to Kelly. The crime ended up in one of these professional reference service databases.[5] Since these services are not covered by FCRA, they do not have to let an individual review their own record. Nor do they have a method to rectify incorrect information. Kelly had to plead and endure several years of hardship until this matter was straightened out.

At least Kelly's tale eventually had a happy ending. Ms. Givens has another case that has not yet ended. Ron Dean was hurt in a construction accident, so he tried to find work in the computer field. He tried for seven years. Companies would be interested at the first interview—and even the second and third. But again, no offers. Dean believes the problem is a case of mistaken identity. He has the same initials and last name as his brother, and their Social Security numbers are one digit apart. His brother has a criminal record.[6]

But Ron Dean cannot confirm that he is being turned down because a database error has confused him with his brother. Companies do not respond because they are not required to show him his record or tell him anything about its contents. He did learn from one potential employer that the problem was in the report it obtained from an "outside" source.

Under the FCRA, you have the right to know what is in your credit report and who has accessed it, and you are entitled to correct inaccurate information. But only three companies are held to this code of fair conduct. There could be hundreds of other companies (depending on how broadly you define this industry) that operate without your knowledge and can cause you harmful repercussions as they did Kelly and Dean.

Ms. Givens did take time to review the guidance the Privacy Rights Clearinghouse provides people in this situation. It suggests you go to the Yellow Pages of your phone book and look under "investigators." If you live in a large metropolitan area, you will find several pages of services with titles such as private investigator, employment background checkers, tenant-screening services, and lost family member searches. Make sure the person you select is experienced in employment background checks. This should be the person's specialty. Confirm the charge—it will probably be over $100. If all goes well, the investigator will have at their disposal the same reference service databases that companies are using. By doing a thorough search, the investigator will be able to confirm and pinpoint the problem if it is an error in the database.[7]

Still, no formal channel for correction exists. And information is being combined all the time to create newly merged databases. So, even though you now know the problem, you still have a trying time ahead of you.

Intensified Privacy Feelings

Because no system of ensuring fair play is available and little understanding or awareness of the reference service industry exists, rumors and misinformation about these companies circulate. This occurred to Lexis-Nexis, a unit of the Reed Elsevier plc group, when it attempted to introduce a new product, P-Trak, to its commercial customers.

Lexis-Nexis pioneered the field of computer-assisted legal research back in the 1970s. It is now the largest commercial database service with over one billion documents and over 7,000 databases. These databases are principally archival information and cover legal cases, news, finance, and public records.

On June 1, 1996, Lexis-Nexis introduced a new product—P-Trak—which contained millions of records. Each record had a person's name, known alias (this could be a woman's maiden name), up to two prior addresses, month and year of birth, Social Security number, and telephone number. The P-Trak system was available not on the Internet but on a proprietary electronic system. Lexis-Nexis' 740,000 commercial and professional company subscribers had to have proprietary software, an assigned identification number, and a signed contract with Lexis-Nexis to access this new service.

During the first release week, Lexis-Nexis got a tremendous amount of feedback from its customers. Half of them loved the new service and its easy access; but the other half, many from the legal profession, were worried about the inclusion of Social Security numbers. Identity theft and credit card fraud were possibilities when the Social Security number was so readily available. There was enough controversy and client concern that on June 11 at 2 A.M., Lexis-Nexis took out all the Social Security numbers. The new record looked like the sample depicted in figure 2.2, which is a mock-up of a record rather than an actual file.

Records could still be searched by Social Security number, but the number did not show up on the record. What was shown was name, known alias, two previous addresses, current address, phone number, month and year of birth. This is the entire record. Any one person could have more than one file depending on the number of names they have used.

In September, an erroneous e-mail message began circulating. It stated:

> Your name, Social Security number, current address, previous addresses, mother's maiden name, birth date and other personal information are now available to anyone with a credit card through a new Lexis database called P-Trak.[8]

The message also provided an 800 number to call and "opt-out" of the system. Of course the message was inaccurate in several of its statements. For example, Social Security numbers had already been removed, and the information was only available to subscribers.

LEVEL 1 – 1 OF 1 DOCUMENT

* * * THIS DATA IS FOR INFORMATIONAL PURPOSES ONLY * * *

PERSON LOCATOR

Name: EASTER, JAMIE M

Other Name: SMITH, JAMIE M

Current Address: 1521 W HIGH STREET, LUCILLE, OH 45678

Previous Addresses: 1234 LANDWOOD AVENUE APT 22
LUCILLE, OH 45678

2050 MACKEY DRIVE APT 7
JEFFERS, WV 41111

Birth Date: 7/1961

Telephone Number: 221-1836

On File Since: 8/1/1982

FIG. 2.2:

P-Trak Record Sample

Source: Lexis-Nexis. LEXIS®-NEXIS® Screen Captures: Reprinted with permission of LEXIS-NEXIS. Copyright 1998 LEXIS-NEXIS, a division of Reed Elsevier Inc. The information/names provided in the LEXIS-NEXIS search results are fictitious and used for illustrative purposes only. LEXIS and NEXIS are registered trademarks, and the INFORMATION ARRAY logo is a trademark of Reed Elsevier Properties, Inc.

This incorrect message went all over the world to millions and millions of people in a week. Individuals would receive the e-mail message and want to make sure their friends, coworkers, and family knew about the threat to their privacy. The massive circulation in a compressed period of time was the result of intensified concerns about private information on the Internet.

Lexis-Nexis 800 phone lines were flooded with individuals who wanted to opt-out. Somehow the original e-mail message changed slightly and at least four different 800 numbers were used in differing messages. When the calls reached Lexis-Nexis, the people at the other end of the line wanted out for a number of reasons—all connected to privacy. Since people were unfamiliar with reference services and their role, they had serious fears about Lexis-Nexis' actions and services. One armed services caller was severely distressed because he thought P-Trak would pinpoint service men and women on active duty in Bosnia and their homes would be targets for theft.

Even though the e-mail message was incorrect, the public reaction was huge. This strong, unwavering response to services providing personal information on the Internet or other proprietary lines is now to be expected. Similar reactions caused Yahoo to drop its plans to make unlisted phone numbers available online.[9]

Are Reference Services Really Necessary?

There are already reference systems up and operating. The reason Lexis-Nexis created P-Trak in the first place was to compete with Information American and CDB offerings. And these systems do perform, in many cases, important work. Karen Welch from its Government Information Services, has been with Lexis-Nexis for over twelve years. She demonstrated both P-Trak and P-Find, using sample documents to show the systems' usefulness. Let's walk through two typical uses of database information, using mock-ups that do not represent real people or real records.

In a typical situation, a user or customer once having made it through the screening process would log on to the Lexis-Nexis system using the confidential ID and the proprietary software and would see a menu and make a database selection. The people locator services are contained in the finder library menu. Among the people locator services selections are P-Trak and P-Find. P-Trak, containing over 324 million records, is selected (see how such information would appear on your screen in figure 2.3).

P-Trak and Its Use

Once selected, P-Trak can be applied to any number of situations. The situation created here is a parent, a custodial parent, trying to locate the non-custodial parent who has not paid child support. A court order has been issued in Michigan and, using P-Trak, the court is determined to locate him. (Remember, all data is fictitious!) In this case, the non-custodial parent's name is Robert Jones. He has a common name and has moved out of state.

The lawyer or government organization charged with enforcement could use the P-Trak system to locate him. If the lawyer ran a search

Please ENTER the NAME of the file you want to search. To see a description of a file, type its page number and press the ENTER key.

FILES – PAGE 1 of 3 (NEXT PAGE for additional files)

NAME	PG	DESCRIP	NAME	PG	DESCRIP
---------------- F I N D E R			L I B R A R Y ----------------		
---------PEOPLE LOCATOR---------			---------BUSINESS LOCATOR---------		
P-TRAK	1	Nationwide file – 324 million records with previous addresses and alias names	B-FIND	1	Nationwide file of US and Canadian Public and Private Companies
P-FIND	1	Nationwide group file – white pages and household information (xxFIND for individual state files)	---------PROFESSIONAL LOCATOR---------		
			CALIC	2	CA Professional Licenses
			FLLIC	2	FL Professional Licenses
			ILLIC	2	IL Professional Licenses
DCEASE	1	Nationwide file containing Social Security Death Master File	MILIC	2	MI Professional Licenses
			NJLIC	2	NJ Professional Licenses
PILOTS	1	Nationwide Pilots Directory	PALIC	2	PA Professional Licenses
			VALIC	2	VA Professional Licenses
			WILIC	2	WI Professional Licenses
			---------DRIVER LICENSES---------		
			FLDL	2	FL Driver Licenses

FIG. 2.3:

Lexis-Nexis Finder Library

Source: Lexis-Nexis. LEXIS®-NEXIS® Screen Captures: Reprinted with permission of LEXIS-NEXIS. Copyright 1998 LEXIS-NEXIS, a division of Reed Elsevier Inc. The information/names provided in the LEXIS-NEXIS search results are fictitious and used for illustrative purposes only. LEXIS and NEXIS are registered trademarks, and the INFORMATION ARRAY logo is a trademark of Reed Elsevier Properties, Inc.

using a common name like Robert Jones, the lawyer would end up with far too many records. But the custodial parent knows the month and year of Jones' birth so the number of records is narrowed down to 26 documents. The other information known is a previous address so this reduces the list to two possibilities. The lawyer is now faced with the problem of figuring out which of the two is the man she is looking for.

This is where being able to search by Social Security number is valuable. The custodial parent knows Robert Jones' Social Security number and the lawyer or government organization uses this to narrow the field. Of course, it could have searched by Social Security number initially. Even though the Social Security number does not appear, it is a search element.

LEVEL 3 – 1 OF 2 DOCUMENTS

* * THIS DATA IS FOR INFORMATIONAL PURPOSES ONLY * * *

PERSON LOCATOR

Name: JONES, ROBERT

Other Name: JONES, BOBBY

Current Address: 1035 HUNTER AVE, KEENE, KY 41111

Previous Addresses: 444 EMMETT ST
SPIVEY, MD 22000

11 MIGHLAND AVE, APT J
LEEDSBURG, OH 43333

Birth Date: 1/1948

Telephone Number: 321-5566

On File Since: 12/11/1994

FIG. 2.4:

Fictitious Robert Jones file

Source: Lexis-Nexis. LEXIS®-NEXIS® Screen Captures: Reprinted with permission of LEXIS-NEXIS. Copyright 1998 LEXIS-NEXIS, a division of Reed Elsevier Inc. The information/names provided in the LEXIS-NEXIS search results are fictitious and used for illustrative purposes only. LEXIS and NEXIS are registered trademarks, and the INFORMATION ARRAY logo is a trademark of Reed Elsevier Properties, Inc.

Now the lawyer or government agency knows where to find the parent to collect the child support payments (see fictitious example in figure 2.4).

How to Use P-Find

P-Find, the other service, is a bit different. It covers 111 million records and is a white page–type directory. In addition it contains aggregate U.S. Census data. A routine use for P-Find would be witness location. To illustrate this database, pretend that an automobile accident in Maryland in late 1994 resulted in a personal injury case. The case has taken a long time to come to trial and now the lawyers are trying to track down eyewitnesses. Given how mobile people are today, one witness, Alan Crane, could have moved several times.

By typing in "Alan Crane" to the P-Find system, the lawyer might retrieve 29 records. She then reviews the records and thinks that of the 29 records, #7 is most likely the witness Alan Crane (see figure 2.5). The lawyer does not need to narrow the field to just one person. Unlike the P-Trak enforcement case previously, the lawyer can contact the most

LEVEL 1 – 7 OF 29 DOCUMENTS

PERSON LOCATOR

* * * THIS DATA IS FOR INFORMATION PURPOSES ONLY * * *

RESIDENT(S)	APPROXIMATE BIRTH DATE
CRANE, ALAN	05/57
CRANE, MARIE (SPOUSE)	09/64

ADDRESS: 44 PLEASANT ST, PARKSVILLE, PA 12345

TELEPHONE NUMBER: 115-123-9876

DWELLING-TYPE: SINGLE FAMILY

HOMEOWNER PROBABILITY: 50%

YEAR RESIDENCE FIRST LISTED IN PHONE BOOK: 96

APPROXIMATE HEAD OF HOUSEHOLD (HOH) BIRTH DATE: 05/57

FIG. 2.5: Example of P-Find Sample Record

Source: Lexis-Nexis. LEXIS®-NEXIS® Screen Captures: Reprinted with permission of LEXIS-NEXIS. Copyright 1998 LEXIS-NEXIS, a division of Reed Elsevier Inc. The information/names provided in the LEXIS-NEXIS search results are fictitious and used for illustrative purposes only. LEXIS and NEXIS are registered trademarks, and the INFORMATION ARRAY logo is a trademark of Reed Elsevier Properties, Inc.

promising person to see whether she has the correct one. People are usually willing to respond to a request that they be a witness. If #7 is not the witness the lawyer is seeking, she can then call others on the list.

As shown in these examples, the professional reference services provide information that lawyers and government agencies need. The Secret Service uses several database services to investigate counterfeit currency and financial crimes, including credit card fraud. In 1996 it ran over 64,000 inquiries. Journalists, who rely on speed and accuracy, use the services to locate potential interviews, find out more about the subjects of the stories, and to uncover false information.

Nevertheless, professional reference services' use of private information is a serious control concern. Knowing what information of yours they have, how they are using it, and how to correct inaccuracies are all elements of good business practices and codes of fair conduct. Perhaps if the clients of these companies were individuals, they would be able to use their economic or market strength to change the practice, but this is not the case. A remedy is necessary or the public will continue to react forcefully to reference service activities. But will change be government-imposed or industry self-regulated?

WHITE PAGES—LOOK-UPS YOU CAN USE

While Lexis-Nexis and others sell their services to professional organizations and businesses, some reference services sell directly to consumers. These services, called look-up services or the white pages industry, publish what is freely available and publicly disclosed. This is the information you could find in a telephone book and, like in a telephone book, usually doesn't include unlisted numbers. This limits the sample because unlisted numbers average 33 percent of telephone numbers in any given area, and 50 percent in Washington, D.C., and parts of California. You used one of these services, Infoseek, to conduct your Personal Privacy Profile in Chapter 1.

Most of these services provide telephone numbers and addresses; some will find e-mail addresses; and a couple will even provide directions to the address for you. But only a few white page directories allow a *reverse look-up,* which is just what it sounds like. You input a phone number and you obtain the names of all the people using that phone number and their addresses. So if you are a parent and want to make sure your son or daughter really *is* living alone, this is the system for you. Or if you are dating a man or woman whom you suspect may be married, it is a possible way to verify marital status.

For many services, a reverse look-up offers information the telephone book may not; it goes beyond the publicly disclosed information. Even though the technology can effortlessly recalculate the requested information, it troubles some people that it is available. Even more troubling are the white page services that combine publicly disclosed information (like the telephone book) with public records. State and local governments may have this information available on the Internet. But a great leap takes place when you can go to a reference service on the Internet and find out about any state's records.

One such service, the American Information Network (www.ameri.com) has a fee-based service on individual and consumer backgrounds that includes:

- Driver's license histories
- Statewide and countywide criminal records
- Federal criminal records
- Civil case records
- Consumer public filings (bankruptcies, judgments, tax liens)
- Consumer credit reports
- Workman's compensation records
- Professional license verifications
- Education verifications

If you want to make sure the new nanny you've hired does not have a reckless driving record, this service will provide the answer. For a few dollars, it will give you a three- to seven-year driving record, complete with everything, including the organ donor status.[10] This was once information you had to physically go to a government building or office to get. Now it's available to anyone with a modem and a computer.

PERSONAL PRIVACY PROFILE NO. 2

Let's extend your Personal Privacy Profile and at the same time demonstrate just how easy one can obtain these vast quantities of sensitive information. Among the most comprehensive sources of public information on the Web is KnowX (www.knowX.com). When you arrive at the site you will be dazzled by all the information you can obtain. It will take you a while to read through all your choices. There is also a charge for certain kinds of information at key times during the day. Since you are looking for public filings, bankruptcies, judgments, and liens, you might be able to search for free, especially if you do your search during off hours.

Again, a caution for those using the Internet for the first time. Web sites are occasionally down or not functioning, or the Web operators may have improved their Web site and it may look different than described here. You should still be able to work your way through the site; it will just take slightly more time.

Just as you did in chapter 1, log on to your Internet service provider and go to the Internet's World Wide Web. Type this address into the "Location" or "Go To" line: http://www.knowX.com.

When you arrive at the KnowX site, scroll down the screen. You will see general information about price lists and a brief write-up about Information America, the company that supplies much of the data. Further down is Timesaver Multiple, which are combined databases available for Web searching. One mentioned under the category of Assets will search real-estate, stock, aircraft ownership, and watercraft records. Next in your scrolling you will find Nationwide Public Records. There are 20 of these single-topic databases, including death records, real property foreclosures, and professional licenses to mention a few. You are almost to the final category: Free Single State Searches. These are available from 6 P.M. to 11 A.M. on Monday through Friday and all day on Saturday and Sunday.

Click on Free Search. You will be asked where you learned about KnowX; then you can place your request. You select a state and the categories you want checked out—liens, lawsuits, judgments, and bankruptcy. Do the search on yourself and see what comes up. Even if you have no adverse court records, you will be able to sort through tons of files fairly quickly to see what is recorded about you. This information is essentially your past. When you are Web-browsing on the Internet and visiting Web sites and home pages, information is being collected about you in real time. Your present activities are being monitored and stored through a number of technologies. As with reference services—the information collectors are quiet and invisible.

3

THE CYBER GATHERERS AND YOU

Cyberspace is different. Whether you're on a private system, in a chat room, or on a Web site visit, the rules and clues you depended on in the physical world no longer exist. This chapter looks at the Internet and pinpoints where your personal information is exposed. It describes the exposure, particularly if it is technological; assesses just how vulnerable you are; and includes in the discussion good Internet practices and habits that you can adopt. You'll also learn what a "cookie" is and see how one works on your computer through the final Personal Privacy Profile exercise.

RULES AND CLUES YOU NEED IN CYBERSPACE

From 1994 to 1998 the number of people using the Internet expanded from three million (most in the United States) to 100 million worldwide. Some experts believe that one billion people may be connected to the Internet by 2005. All of these users will be part of a radically new way of interacting.

Cyberspace—where machines talk to and exchange information with other machines—is the established venue of the Internet. The type of information transmitted through cyberspace is the same in every transaction. It includes the IP (Internet protocol) address, which is a string of numbers that looks something like this: 129.63.54.79. Each computer has an IP number. The current Internet, including the large number of reserved IP numbers for official purposes, has available 255^{4th} numbers—more than enough to go around until the next generation Internet comes along.

In addition to the IP number, the machine provides its domain address for the computer's e-mail and Internet activities. This is not your e-mail address, but it is related. If the computer was at the Department of Commerce's National Institute of Standards and Technology, for example, the domain address would be nist.gov. Note it's the computer with the domain address and IP number, not the person operating the computer. Domain addresses fall into several set categories, which are reviewed in figure 3.1.

Like everything about the Internet, the number of domain names is growing rapidly. The number of names registered in the domain name system grew from 26,000 in July 1993 to 1.3 million four years later. In 1995 there were just over 27,000 top level commercial (.com) domain names assigned. Two and a half years later, commercial domain names numbered over 764,000.

Computers also exchange the current date, time, and the browser they are using. All this happens instantly when one computer connects to another. However, this instant relaying of information does not necessarily tell you anything about the person sitting at the computer.

Cyberspace– Not the World As You Know It

When you connect to someone in cyberspace, you cannot see or hear the person at the other computer. In cyberspace, there are no faces, no voices. For example, you may find yourself in an Internet chat room—a

Domain Names

Addresses on the Internet have "zone" name extensions. These exist so you can look at an address and know what type of organization it represents or what country the message comes from. Here are some examples:

.com	U.S. commercial business
.jp	Japan
.edu	U.S. college or university
.uk	United Kingdom
.gov	Government agency
.au	Australia
.mil	Military/Department of Defense
.int	International group like NATO
.net	Company running large networks
.org	Nonprofit organizations

FIG. 3.1:
Domain Categories

place where people engage in conversation by sending messages to each other. There are people in the chat room just "listening," not participating in the conversation. Unlike in a literal room, where you could see the silent listeners, on the Internet you are blind to what they look like and even that they are there at all. They may be too shy to talk or are trying to find out whether the conversation appeals to them. They may be law enforcement officials looking for signs of criminal activity, or they may be gathering e-mail addresses and key words for a marketing campaign.

Going one step further, you may discover that the people with whom you are chatting are not necessarily who they say they are. The fellow going by the name of "Warrior" could be a 73-year-old grandfather or a 14-year-old schoolgirl. Don't count on any chat room participants being the gender, age, or anything they claim. Such fooling occurs regularly in Internet conversations.

Places are not what we are used to in the physical world either. Leslie Byrne, former director of the U.S. Office of Consumer Affairs, uses this illustration. If you buy a Rolex watch from a street vendor and it stops working the next day, you know the place you bought it and you know what to expect. The same is true if you used your credit card at the Greek restaurant down the street. The next day, if you were called by the credit card company asking about some unusual charges, you would know where to check. Not so in cyberspace. The Web site where you used your credit card to buy a Rolex may not be a legitimate business. You may have just given your credit card to a place and to people you will never find again.

This lack of geography is one thing with which law enforcement officials and the Department of Defense have struggled. Computer hackers visit secret installations and defense databases by having their computers log on to other computers and become part of the second computer's system. When the hacker visits the secret database, the hacker appears to be from the second computer. When intrusions are noted, officials have the IP from the second computer and no information about the original computer or the hacker.

Sometimes, to make sure he remains undetectable, a hacker will travel through several computers, thus disguising himself effectively. You will experience geographic anonymity when you take a laptop computer on a business trip and dial into your server or local area network at the office. As you send e-mail messages, your address remains constant. It does not matter whether you are in Phoenix or Paris. This lack of geographic certainty occurs in e-mail addresses and Web sites. While many people in cyberspace are who they say they are and come from the place they claim, the bad guys don't.

Not only are rules and clues different on the Internet; it is a very nosy place. When you are signing on to an Internet service, visiting Web sites, or chatting or participating in newsgroups, your personal information is exposed countless times. Each time, you have a reason for the exposure. After reviewing the exposure points, you can consider whether those reasons make sense. More importantly, you can determine in which areas you feel comfortable participating.

GATEWAYS TO THE INTERNET SERVICE PROVIDERS

Unless you are accessing the Internet from work or college and using a local area network, you probably have signed up with an online service provider (OSP). These are the big guys that not only provide connections to the Internet, but content environments as well. These environments could be chat rooms, shopping malls, or bulletin boards. Each service provider controls its online environment from connection to content. Four companies fit this description: Microsoft, Compuserve, Prodigy, and America Online (AOL). AOL is the largest OSP with approximately 11 million members.

These OSPs also meet the definition of ISP (Internet Service Providers). ISPs vary in size and range of capability but all connect individuals or businesses to the Internet. The ISP category contains 4,500–5,000 companies, and the number is growing.

The ISP will ask you for information necessary to set up an account. Usually this happens right online. The online service provider will ask for your information beyond name, address, and credit card number. If you want to know why they are requesting additional information, ask them.

Using and Being Used by ISPs and OSPs

Many online services and Internet service providers tell customers how they use the information they collect. The service's policy on use of personal information should be part of the agreement you are asked to review—either as a separate document or on the service's Web site. Many services share their customer lists with other companies that want to sell products and services to online consumers. If the service is following the Interactive Services Association (ISA) guidelines, it should disclose its policies and let you "opt-out" if you do not want personal information shared with third parties. Some online services offer this option as part of the signup process. Others permit you to state your marketing preferences in a separate area where you can make choices about how your online sessions will be set up.[11]

For example, when you register with AOL, you are asked to make a number of choices. One is your preference regarding marketing. AOL clearly states that the company makes mailing lists available and provides its subscribers the opportunity to "opt-out." Then, every time you sign on to AOL, you have another chance to reconsider.

Your service will have your signup information. While you are a member, it will also monitor the amount of time you use the system and how you use it. This may be done for billing customers or companies that provide online activities and get paid by the online service based on usage. Or it may be to help the OSP develop new services and upgrade existing ones. Typically the information is aggregated or pooled. In other words, the service knows 10,000 customers visited a certain site, but it doesn't keep track of which customers used it. This monitoring takes place more often with the online service providers than with the Internet service providers.

How to Access the Internet

Once you are signed up, you select a username. You can adopt a username that is a variation of your name (chris peterson or cpeterson) or you can create an online name that bears no resemblance to your real name. For example, a well-respected moderator of newsgroup on Internet abuse policy goes by "fluffy," and a prominent medical researcher uses "germ." It is this name that shows up when you send messages or participate in other activities. So the username will combine with the online service for your entire e-mail address. If the online service was AOL, the address would be cpeterson@aol.com.

Many of the bigger commercial services provide directories of their members or member profiles. You decide whether you want to be listed and what sorts of information about yourself you want to provide. The directory helps identify people with common interests, but it also releases information about you that can be seen by many. It may encourage strangers to send you e-mail. If either situation makes you uncomfortable, don't participate.

In addition to selecting a username, you will select a password. Be cautious. Don't select a name similar to yours, or your favorite football team or family member name. Easy-to-guess passwords might give someone access to your online account. The safest passwords are those that mix letters

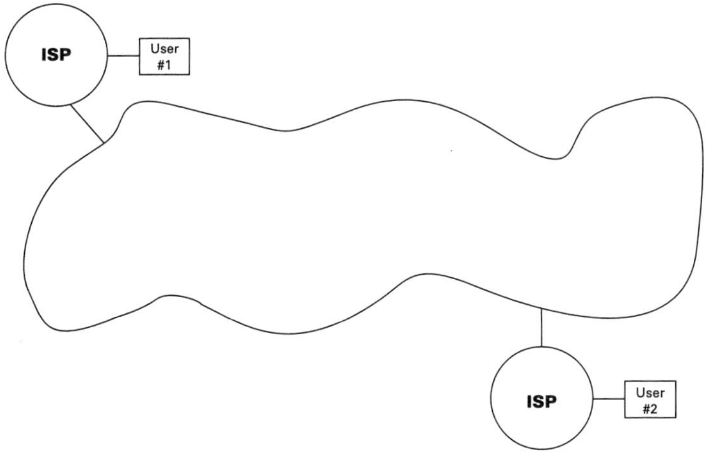

FIG. 3.2:
Opportunities for Exposure

and numbers, that are six characters or more, and that don't represent a word in any language, whether spelled forward or backward.[12] Be vigilant!

Some scam artists pose as representatives of your online service. They call themselves systems administrators or customer representatives or other titles connoting an official capacity with the ISP. These imposters may send you a message asking for either your password or your credit card number. The message may even sound very official. Never respond to such requests. Remember your service already has this information. In fact, report the incident to your service and send them a copy of the message!

It is now time to venture into the Internet and see the different places you can go and how much personal information you reveal to get there. Figure 3.2 is a view of the Internet and the activities that can take place there. We'll examine e-mail; visit Web sites; join chat rooms; and learn about LISTSERV, bulletin boards, news groups, and search engines.

E-MAIL—WHAT IS IT?

Figure 3.2 illustrates one Internet user (User 1) sending an e-mail message to another (User 2). User 1 and User 2 both have ISPs (Internet service providers). E-mail is not the equivalent of a letter going through the postal system. Your letter sent via the postal system is in a sealed envelope and is protected by harsh laws against anyone (U.S. Postal Service or next-door neighbor) opening your mail. A postcard is a more apt analogy for e-mail. The only people likely to see your message besides Users 1 and 2 are the systems administrators for both ISPs. Like a postcard, the systems administrators *could* read it; generally, this doesn't happen and e-mail remains private—unless a third party gets it.

This happens when you accidentally type in an incorrect address or when the recipient of your message decides to forward your message to others. Unlike regular mail, which would require the intended receiver to copy the message, address new envelopes, affix additional postage, and make a trip to the mailbox, forwarding e-mail requires a simple click of the mouse to send your message to many unintended recipients. Remember the e-mail message about Lexis-Nexis' P-Trak system. It went to millions of people in less than one week. So, you may want to think twice about communicating very sensitive information about yourself or others.

A third party could be a hacker or scam artist who has penetrated the mail host. One tool the hacker could use is a "sniffer," which is akin to network analyzers used to diagnose problems with the network connectivity. Unlike a network analyzer searching for information about connectivity, the sniffer cruises the Internet in search of specific information like passwords and e-mail addresses. Once the hacker has your password and address, the hacker can masquerade as you and do considerable damage. These situations are infrequent and for the most part, e-mail used sensibly is private.

VISITING A WEB SITE

Visiting a Web site offers many opportunities for Web site operators and others to gather information surreptitiously. Over 200 million Web sites are now part of the Internet and more show up every day. Each is different in its purpose, presentation, and strategy for collecting personal information. When you log on to a Web site, the site immediately obtains your IP, domain name, time, date, and browser—the standard information gathered by any computer talking to another computer. Such information allows the site to count how many visitors arrive at the site. The site may then monitor and collect other information from your visit. "Transactional information," the broad term for this category of information, has several elements. Probably most interesting is the part of transactional information called click-stream data or mouse tracks. This is navigational information about your visit to the Web site. Click-stream data includes what hyperlinks you clicked on, in what order, and how long you looked at any one screen. Without your knowledge, and whether you care or not, the site records every aspect of your visit. Generally the data is statistical in nature and used by the Web servers for maintaining the system, auditing, and performing other system functions.

Web sites did not initially have the ability to track visitors. The privacy invasion technology was limited to registering the IP information of visitors. To learn more about the visitors and what interested them, Web site operators had to ask by using surveys, registration forms, and questionnaires. But operators recognized that people were reluctant to voluntarily answer personal questions.

Click-through information was one of the original technologies for obtaining information by using technology. I/PRO, an Internet startup, rolled out a product called I/Code. I/Code deals with the dilemma of Web site visitors wanting to preserve their privacy as they enjoy the information and entertainment the site provides and site managers wanting feedback on the site's usage so they can tailor the experience in terms of content and ads. Before I/Code, sites relied on making personal background information their price of admission. I/Code counted whenever somebody clicked on a banner (the advertising strip on top of many Web pages) and came to the sponsor's site. Further, click-through performance could be tracked in real time to help site managers and advertisers refine their messages.[13]

As with ISP monitoring, click-stream information is statistical. And it does tell a lot about you. It tells which pages you looked at and how long you looked as well as which topics didn't interest you. Transactional data, including click-stream information, in this new media is more detailed and descriptive than ever before. The data by itself, while revealing, is not tied to you as an individual. Even aggregated it is still capable of revealing much.

Registering has not disappeared. Many sites still ask visitors to register and in the process request personal information. This creates a situation in which the click-stream information can be connected with your personal identifying registration—all without your knowledge. This information could even be married with data from powerful reference services such as those discussed in chapter 2, which further increases the power of the invasion technologies.

The Electronic Privacy Information Center (EPIC) in Washington, D. C., surveyed 100 popular sites to determine their personal information collection practices. On June 5, 1997, the center studied the top 100 sites listed by www.100hot.com. This site lists only Web sites—not browsers, ISPs, colleges, or adult sites. Of the 100 sites surveyed, 49 collected personal information through online registrations, mailing lists, surveys, user profiles, and order-fulfillment requirements.[14]

How to Preserve Your Privacy at a Web Site

Very few Web sites explain how the information they collect would be used. Only 17 of the 100 surveyed had privacy policies or statements; and many of those were difficult to locate. A good privacy policy statement should tell the visitor:

- What information is being collected
- Why the information is being collected
- How the information will be used

Another element of a good privacy policy statement is a discussion of what steps will be taken in cases of improper disclosure. With this information clearly explained, the visitor can decide whether or not to provide personal information. Privacy policies or statements are showing up more frequently since the 1997 EPIC survey, as their desirability and popularity increase.

Even if you chose not to fill out the registration form or survey, all sites let you access at least the first screen of the home page. This makes good sense. The Web site manager *wants* people to visit. Registration often dissuades people from spending time at the site and learning about the product or process. The example in the EPIC survey compared cyberspace to the physical world aptly: "In the physical world, we note that very few stores require the collection of personal information before allowing someone to enter."[15]

Watch Out for Cookies

In this survey 24 sites enabled "cookies." Like collecting of transactional information, this practice is invisible to the user. In this case, none of the sites that enabled cookies told the visitor that information about the visitor was being place in the visitor's system. But what is a cookie? Figure 3.3 defines and discusses this practice.

A cookie is a file that is transferred from the site you are visiting, through your Web browser, to your hard drive. The cookie lets the Web site manager track your activities while you visit the site. Many cookies expire at the end of a visit; but some last for years. Those that last contain a code that lets the site recognize you on your return visits. This may benefit you in two ways.

First, it may let you skip the registration process. The *New York Times* Web site enables a cookie on your computer so you don't need to register or for that matter remember your password on repeat visits. In addition, it can enhance what the Web manager knows about you and let him or her create content and information that you will find attractive. When you return for a visit, the cookie can remind the site that you are from Sweden and display the content or ad in Swedish for you.

Although cookies have positive aspects, that doesn't alter the fact that they are sneaky. You can get rid of cookies yourself by changing the options on your browser. Or, consider installing specialized software that will alert you to cookies and give you the choice whether or not to disable them. These programs include Cookie Pal 1.0 (www.kburra.com), InternetJunkbuster 2.0 (www.junkbusters.com), and PGP cookie.cutter (www.pgp.com).

What Is a Cookie?

Some Web sites transfer a file, generally referred to as a "cookie," to the hard drive of your computer to let them track your activities on their Web site and sometimes other places on the Internet. A code in the cookie file lets the Web site know that you are a particular user, but it won't know such personal information as your real name and address unless you have specifically provided it at the Web site or have set your preferences in your browser to provide that information.

If you visit a Web site more than once, a cookie file will let it recognize that you are a repeat visitor so that it can provide you with shortcuts or faster access to the areas you've used before. Some Web site operators also use cookie files to learn more about your interests and online habits. In addition, some operators use them to manage the advertising messages you see on their Web sites.

Newer versions of many browser software packages enable you to specify that you do not want to receive cookie files. In addition, some programs will notify you when a Web site is about to deposit a cookie file. These choices can usually be found under headings such as "Preferences" or "Options."

You can check to see if any cookie files have been placed on your computer by looking for a file on your hard drive labeled "cookies.txt" if you use a PC, or a file labeled "magic cookies" if you use a Macintosh computer. You can delete these files from your computer if you wish.

FIG. 3.3:
What Is a Cookie?

Source ISA Project Open, http://www.isa.net/project-open

CHAT ROOMS AND BULLETIN BOARDS

It is time to leave Web surfing and move to a more social environment. Starting with chat rooms and moving to bulletin boards, the array of personal information collectors broadens. In your Web site visits, usually only the Web site managers are interested in you and have access to your personal information. In this more genial arena, companies or individuals may be seeking to learn more about you.

Chat Rooms—Where Humans and Non-Humans Can Talk

A chat room is a place furnished by a Web site or your ISP that allows online conversation, where you "talk" with other users from anywhere on the Internet. Chat rooms let a group of people communicate simultaneously online by typing messages to one another. When you type a message, everyone in the "room" is able to see it. You can find permanent chat rooms devoted to certain topics. If you have an interest in antiques, genealogy, or any of a thousand topics, there is a chat room for you. There are also informal chat rooms to which a group that wants to talk together can move or create. Such rooms are open continuously. Many Internet users enjoy the social aspects of chat more than any other rewards found while surfing the Net.

Advertisers like having chat rooms incorporated in their sites because they can lace the discussions with promotional messages that—if they are subtle enough—will not appear to be direct advertising. In the future, non-human participants may inhabit chat rooms too. Ad "robots" that will listen in chat rooms are under development by Black Sun Interactive Inc. of San Francisco. When these machines recognize key phrases, they will respond with a product advertisement. So if "My house is dirty" were typed in, you might get a response like, "Hi, I'm Dusty. Would you like to learn more about Black & Decker's Dustbuster?"[16] Tests are still underway. In the first chat-room test, Dusty didn't announce that he was a salesman until conversation had been underway for five or ten minutes. People were insulted. Now, in trials, the robot identifies himself immediately.

A Laugh Whenever You Need It

People in a chat room know the e-mail addresses of those sending messages during the session. Unless the conversations are stored, the participants are the only ones with this information. In bulletin boards (also known as newsgroups), your personal information may be at greater risk.

Bulletin boards and newsgroups differ from chat rooms in one significant way—*when* the interaction occurs. In a chat room, the interaction happens simultaneously, when everyone is together. This is not the case for a bulletin board or newsgroups. A bulletin board in cyberspace is essentially the same as one in the physical world; people post messages in a public place on the Internet whenever they please. If you want to read the message, you don't have to be there when it is posted. The posting will remain until it's convenient for you to look at it.

Like chat rooms, bulletin boards are created for those with specific interests. Thousands of topic groups exist—on politics, hobbies, business, and even favorite TV shows. One of the most widely read features is the selected jokes.

Deja News (www.dejanews.com) is the host of a number of discussion groups. In the food newsgroup, for example, you can read messages from people looking for new recipes, wanting to share recipes, or wanting to talk about low-fat cooking. One woman announced she wanted to buy a freezer and did not know whether to get an upright or the footlocker style. Advice poured in with tidbits about energy efficiency being worse in the upright style countered by people having strained their backs from getting frozen food out of the footlocker style. Several groups focus on the subject of privacy; these include talk.politics.crypto, a discussion of encryption policy, and alt.privacy and comp.org.eff.talk, sites at which general discussion on privacy issues occurs.

Instead of going to a public bulletin board on the Internet, you can subscribe to an electronic mailing list or LISTSERV. An individual would e-mail a message to a central location, majordomo@name of group. The message would then be sent out to all the subscribers of that mailing list. LISTSERVs are developed based on interest areas. To explore the possibilities, visit www.Liszt.com.

Whether on a LISTSERV or bulletin board, anyone at anytime can obtain the e-mail address of the participants.

SEARCH AND FIND

Search engines index each Web site, following all hyperlinks carefully to note all the links. Ones you may have heard of are Alta Vista, Hot Bot, Lycos, and Deja News. If you would like to gather up e-mail addresses for a mailing of unsolicited e-mail (also called junk mail or "spam"), you could use a search engine to get you to a newsgroup and gather all the addresses. These e-mail addresses are then sent electronic junk mail—spam.

SPAM

Privacy can take on different shapes. The *concrete* concern about unwanted or unknown people having access to sensitive information about you is not the issue with spam. Spam is a *control* concern. Control concerns are based on a desire to understand and to decide what happens to your information. In the case of spam, you lose control and gain annoyance.

One piece of junk mail may not be irritating, but lots of junk mail certainly is. One gentleman saved the junk mail he had received for nine months. He found he was getting about one piece of junk every two days. After nine months, he was receiving about six junk mailings every day. It didn't take a lot of mathematical knowledge for him to realize that he will have received approximately 753 pieces of junk mail by the end of a year.

How did the people who send out junk mail get this man's address? It came from harvesting e-mail addresses from Deja News, Usenet, chat rooms, classified ads, user directories, and newsgroups. There was a time when even AOL profiles were used to get addresses. If either you or your child have your own home page or Web site that lists an e-mail address, that address will be harvested.

Think about that term: "harvesting." It brings up a positive image of a farmer planting seeds on his land and nurturing crops. But Jason Catlett, president of Junkbusters, thinks "scavenging" is a better term. Spammers are trolling everywhere on the Internet for addresses. Once they have yours, you can expect two kinds of messages. The first comes from amateurs and is readily recognizable. Here is a sample of an opening line:

Forgive the intrusion, but Im compelld to tell you how to make a lot of money.

It's marginally literate, riddled with spelling errors and full of false claims. All these elements are thrown together in an incoherent presentation that nobody who reads it would fall for.

Almost all major online service companies have strict policies against spamming, and are vigilant in terminating accounts that violate their terms of service. So small-time spanners don't keep it up for long. Sadly, even though many get discouraged and quit, as a group they are being born in increasing numbers. And the spammers who survive do so by learning to cover their tracks or by getting software or a "spam factory" to cover their tracks, making them much harder to stop.

This sort of spam is a step up from the amateur version. There is more of it and it has more diversity. Most such spam announcements fall into one of the following categories:

- Chain letters
- Pyramid schemes, including Multilevel Marketing (MLM)
- Other "Get Rich Quick" or "Make Money Fast" (MMF) schemes
- Offers for phone sex lines and ads for pornographic Web sites
- Offers of software for collecting e-mail addresses and sending unsolicited commercial e-mail (UCE)
- Offers of bulk e-mail services for sending UCE
- Stock offerings for unknown startup corporations
- Quack health products and remedies
- Illegally pirated software ("Warez")[17]

Spam Is Fraud

As a general rule, believe nothing you read in spam. The reputation of spam is so bad and so far-reaching, even legitimate companies are worried about approaching their customers via e-mail because they may be categorized with spammers. The Direct Marketing Association says that only 10 percent of its members market by e-mail, even though 86 percent are actively using the Internet and the World Wide Web. The 10 percent that use e-mail do so to revisit existing clients.

Why is the Internet such a fruitful place for spam factories? The biggest reasons are opportunity and cost. Opportunity exists because of the vast market of potential buyers on the Internet. With 10,000 new people logging on every day, spammers have a lot of prospects and can reach out to many of them at very reasonable rates.

One piece of physical direct mail costs about $1. This includes time and materials such as paper and postage. When you spend $1 a piece, you naturally limit the number of items you send because the price escalates quickly. For the same $1, with a 28.8 dial-up connection and a PC, you can send 10,000 pieces of spam. And the receiver or the ISP ends up paying for it.

In the physical world, the mailer buys the stamp. In the electronic world, the receiver does. So, you may pay directly for each piece of e-mail you get. Or you may have a flat-rate provider (one that charges $10.95 or $19.95 a month). In this case, the ISP pays for the spam. If the ISP gets too much, it has to increase its costs. So in the end, it comes back to you.

ISPs do what they can to control the spam situation and protect their customers, but this is very difficult. Spam uses a very precious commodity, their CPU (central processing unit) time. Bandwidth is an issue too. ISPs purchase bandwidth (their connection with the rest of the Internet) based on their projected usage. They calculate projected usage based on their customers and what they will need. Spam adds to this formula. It increases usage without bringing value to the customers. The smaller ISPs cope by having customers deal with slower Internet access or by raising rates.

Even the large systems struggle. AOL gets about 15 million messages a day into its system. Between 5 percent to 30 percent of it is spam, depending on the day of the week; AOL representatives believe it hovers closer to 30 percent. In any case, the cost to the system is huge.

Why don't we just electronically reply to the e-mail and ask the spammer to take us off the list? Because spammers hide. While they may include a post office box or an 800 number, they forge the headers of messages, making the message appear to have come from somewhere else. Maine Internetworks, Inc. was a victim of this sort of act. The spam sender, a company called Master Graphics, had hidden the e-mail address from the recipients of the unsolicited advertisement by routing the mailing through Maine Internetworks (Mint.net) without its permission. The hundreds of recipients were angry and responded with a flurry of e-mail letting Master Graphics know how they felt. Sadly, Mint.net was the one who got the message. This message cost it system bandwidth, system resources, and time.[18] And such spamming happens every day.

Sometimes you may encounter a false header, one you cannot track to a source. In November of 1997, a mass e-mailing for a program called Stealth Mass Mailer was sent by Fred@nowhere.com. The message promised a system that could forge headers easily. It said: "Here are just a few features of the Stealth Mass Mailer. Forge the header, message ID, [and] ISPs will spin their wheels; add a bogus, authenticated sender to the header, add a complete bogus received from, received by line with real time date stamp and recipient to the header; does not require that a valid property account be entered in order to send your mailings; easy to use, easy to operate."

These forged return addresses do protect spammers from violent responses. Violent responses or retaliations are called "flaming." George Nemeyer operates Tigerden Internet Services, a small not-for-profit ISP in Dayton, Ohio. He reviewed a disturbing piece of spam on their system. Part of the advertisement, in this case a pyramid scheme, was this: "Note to flamers, don't do it. We will comply with all and respect all remove requests, but if we are flamed, we will flame you 1,000 times as much and we will e-mail three million people with a questionable item with your return e-mail address. We want respect as much as anyone else. So if you give it, you shall receive it."

The attitude of spammers seems to be—this is a wonderful way to make money (even if it is fraud) and don't tamper with us. This view may not be universal. In April of 1997, five of the largest unsolicited e-mail companies, including Sanford Wallace's Cyberpromotions, formed a group called the Internet E-mail Marketing Council. The goals were to develop a code of ethics and best practices for the spam industry. So far, little progress has been made.

While self-regulation may not be making progress, several court cases have been successful. AOL was victorious in a suit it filed in October 1997 in Alexandria, Virginia, against Over the Air Equipment Inc. Over the Air Equipment Inc. is a Las Vegas company that sends spam messages promoting adult-oriented Web sites. A federal court ruled against the sex-oriented e-mail company, requiring it to pay damages as well as halt its messages to AOL members. It also has suits against Squeaky Clean Marketing and Cyber Services both of Dallas, Georgia, for ignoring AOL's request to stop sending its users unsolicited mail.[19] Bigfoot Partners, L.P., is using the courts too. Bigfoot's target is CyberPromotions and their CEO, Sanford Wallace. It has a 13-count suit in U.S. District Court for the Southern District of New York alleging CyberPromotions repeated a white pages directory, called Bigfoot, and then harvested its addresses. This is strictly prohibited in the user agreement.[20]

Protecting Yourself from Spam

The courts may be too slow to handle the flood of electronic come-ons. Other options, including blacklisting, filtering software, and legislation, are under consideration. Until the problem is brought under control, you can minimize your vulnerability by considering these ideas:

1. Be careful in chat rooms, newsgroups, and other categories mentioned through which your e-mail address is exposed.
2. Check the trends. If you participate in a certain discussion group then receive unsolicited junk mail a day or two later, you'll know the connection. Some groups and mailing lists may generate more spam than others.
3. Once you're the recipient of spam, treat it appropriately. Whenever possible, just delete—before reading the message. You can identify pieces to delete from the subjects and the e-mail addresses. When you get a message with a certain flavor, such as "opportunity@ ___.com,"

delete it immediately. You have not missed anything. The same holds true for subjects following the themes of money and sex; they are candidates for the trash as well. Money subjects such as "Make Money at Home" and sex topics beginning with "Adults Only" are easily eliminated. Doing so will save you time and aggravation.

PERSONAL PRIVACY PROFILE NO. 3

The third Personal Privacy Profile exercise will demonstrate how a cookie works. The cookie demonstration is done on the Center for Democracy and Technology site, http://www.cdt.org. When you arrive at the site, look at the left-hand column, at the heading "privacy." Click on this and look to the left on the next screen for the heading "About the privacy demo." The final screen, in the center, is a shadow box with an eye and these words: CDT Privacy Demonstration. One final click and you will see the cookie at work. You not only see the initial effect of a cookie but get to see what happens in repeated visits. To return directly to the demonstration, enter this address: http://www.13x.com/cgi-bin/cdt/snoop.pl.

With this background on the privacy invasions of the Internet and the secret stores of personal information held by reference services, you can now apply your knowledge to your life on the Internet—at work and at home.

4

IS NOTHING SACRED? YOUR PRIVACY AT WORK AND HOME

The world is within your reach at work and home because of the Internet. But at each juncture lie certain risks. This chapter notes when your personal information and sometimes your physical well-being are in jeopardy. At work from finding the perfect job to your daily duties, you will be cautioned about seemingly harmless actions that could put you at risk. Your enjoyment of online shopping and socializing will increase if you can lessen the likelihood of theft or stalkers. Good habits and practices are listed to maximize the fun and convenience to be enjoyed online. Awareness and good habits can ensure you will reap the positive aspects of Internet working and playing.

THE INTERNET FOR FUN AND PROFIT

Whether working at the office or shopping and socializing in your free time, the Internet can increase your productivity and your pleasure. The tools of the Internet permit communications with the person in the office down the hall or in the remote field site thousands of miles away. E-mail lets companies make sure everyone knows what is going on and speeds up daily transactions. The Internet and World Wide Web give company representatives new information sources to identify opportunities, reach customers, and learn what the competitors are up to.

When at home, tired from a hard day's work, you can relax by shopping at electronic malls and seeing the vast variety of items for sale. Should something catch your eye that would be just perfect, you can buy it with a click or comparison shop for the best price. Or if you wish to pursue your interest in cooking, you can visit a Web site, chat room, or bulletin board to view the latest recipes, learn about new appliances, and participate in the debate on the tastiness of sugar free recipes. You can even socialize with the opposite sex and perhaps find the love of your life or just enjoy good conversation.

Workplace privacy starts when you interview for the perfect job. The business environment to which you go every day once you are hired offers tools like e-mail and the World Wide Web. How private are these communications? What access do your employers have to your medical records and personal life?

PASSING TODAY'S REFERENCE CHECKS

When the world was a smaller place, employers would "call around" to get the story on job candidates they were considering. Today, those calls would not reveal much. Companies tell very little about former employees because some have been hit by defamation-related lawsuits. The answers one gets in a reference check do not tell whether the woman an employer is considering for a bank manager position is on parole for larceny. They do not indicate that the school bus driver candidate has a string of DUI arrests. Nor will they point out that the potential day-care worker is a convicted child molester.

So, in addition to determining competency, companies must measure and evaluate the trustworthiness of its new hires. According to Aon Consulting, a Detroit firm that conducts an annual survey on this subject, about 95 percent of U.S. corporations now employ background checks. Companies could conduct this scrutiny on their own but are more likely to seek the help of a reference service.

Companies need to be careful because, over the years, the courts have made it clear that the company is responsible for the actions of the employee. In 1996, the Nevada Supreme Court ruled that the family of a person killed by a security guard at an apartment complex could sue the guard's employer, who had failed to look into the guard's criminal background.[21] Rulings such as this make companies even more cautious, spurring them to check on the driving record, criminal charges or convictions, creditworthiness, and education of every employee from clerk to CEO.

When you are job hunting, expect a background investigation. Know that databases doing the background check can have errors, and be prepared. A starting point is to check your credit report. You can call Trans Union (800) 680-7293; Experian (888) 397-3742; and Equifax (800) 556-4711 to obtain your credit reports. These three credit bureaus are regulated by the FCRA and required to cooperate. Getting your own report enables you to correct any errors in the files the three credit bureaus maintain.

But people will have to keep their fingers crossed if your potential employer is not using a credit bureau. If the employer is using any other company in the family of reference services, you cannot obtain the files that the company has on you. Remember, only the credit bureaus offer this recourse. There is no method to see individual records from other reference services. For general information on your rights, consider visiting Experian's new Web site (www.experian.com). The site has a nice explanation of credit report basics and advice on applying for loans, filing bankruptcy, and repairing credit. Earlier it provided, for a fee, online credit reports. This service has been temporarily suspended.

NO DIGITAL DILLYDALLYING PERMITTED ON THE JOB

Even during the busiest days, an employee's mind will occasionally wander. Sometimes that employee will have his or her computer wander, too,

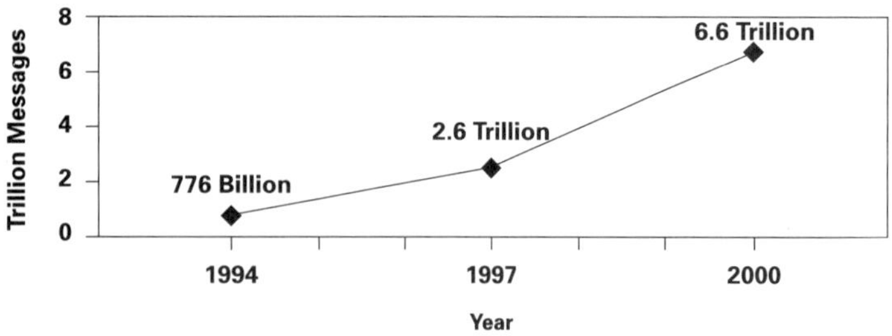

FIG. 4.1:
Number of E-Mail Messages Moving Through U.S.–Based Computer Networks

Source: Time Magazine, *April 21, 1997*

and will check out sites on the World Wide Web that talk about travel to romantic or adventurous lands. From 5 to 40 percent of the time, corporate networks are used during work hours for purposes unrelated to corporate business. Termed "digital dillydallying" by a *Wall Street Journal* report, such wandering on corporate time is a productivity issue for many companies. Nielsen Media Research Inc. conducted an analysis of computer logs and found that employees at International Business Machines Corporation, Apple Computer Inc., and AT&T together visited *Penthouse* magazine's World Wide Web site 12,823 times in a single month. Based on an average visit of 13 minutes, that is more than 347 eight-hour days.[22]

At Compaq's headquarters in Houston, 12 workers were fired for visiting sexually explicit sites on the Internet while at work. The company's objection was not that the sites were sexual; it was the misuse of company resources. Web surfing may be a problem for some employees, but it is not as thorny an issue as e-mail.

Most of us have e-mail at the office. About 40 percent of the U.S. workforce uses it, and the volume of traffic is exploding. In 1994, 776 billion e-mail messages moved through U.S.-based computer networks. By 1997, the number had tripled to 2.6 trillion (see figure 4.1).

Not all the messages sent from office terminals are work-related. Whether a note to a former college roommate or a meeting announcement to fellow PTA members, personal messages are often sent during work hours. And many senders think their communications are private. They are wrong. The case of Shoars v. Epson America, widely reported at the time, is a good example.

In 1989, Alana Shoars joined Epson America, a subsidiary of a giant Japanese electronics manufacturer, as their e-mail administrator. She hoped to encourage the 700 people on the system in her California location to increase their usage of e-mail. She was also charged with expanding the system and connecting the other Epson subsidiaries.

Shoars felt one way to increase usage was to make sure the users understood that e-mail was private. With clearance from her supervisor, she held training classes showing users how to work the system, including instructing users on selecting a password to access e-mail and keeping the password secret. Others would not know your password and could not then look at your e-mail. The password feature, she explained, protected their privacy and the confidentiality of the messages they were sending.

WHOSE E-MAIL IS IT?

In December of 1989, Shoars discovered her supervisor, Robert Hillseth, reading and printing out the electronic mail messages of other employees. She was appalled. Her shock was not only because her supervisor had told her he supported her message of privacy and confidentiality when he apparently felt the opposite; rather, it was the secret nature of his monitoring that she found most upsetting. Later in the week, she spoke about her concerns to her supervisor. Later still, she visited the company CEO. On January 25, 1990, she was called into her supervisor's office. Hillseth accused her of obtaining her own personal MCI Mail account against company policy. She was terminated immediately.

Shoars hired attorney Noel Shipman and filed a class-action suit for invasion of privacy under California statutes. Since there were no laws specifically covering e-mail, the court heard arguments from both sides trying to ascertain whether employees had a right to expect privacy. Shoars felt clearly that they did. If privacy were not important, there wouldn't be passwords. Epson's attorney had a very different point of view. He claimed, "Electronic mail is a business device used in a business environment for a business purpose. There is no other purpose for it. It's sitting on a table provided by the employer with the hardware and the software provided by the employer for only one reason, and that reason is to make the employee more efficient."[23]

On July 31, 1992, the class action suit was denied in the privacy suit. The court found "no sufficient legal or factual basis for extending the right to privacy to cover business-oriented communications." Shoars was disappointed but not surprised. Throughout the hearing, she was concerned that the judge did not understand or use e-mail and consequently would not understand the meaning or value of passwords. She took to signing her correspondence "Alana 'David v. Goliath' Shoars."[24]

Even without this court case, companies have increased their interest and monitoring of employee e-mail. The Society for Human Resource Managers, which has more than 70,000 professional and student members, conducted a random sampling of 3,000 members in December 1995. More than 500 responded to the survey. The findings were:

- E-mail was used by nearly 80 percent of the responding organizations.
- Thirty-six percent of the managers said they access employee e-mail records for business necessity or security.
- Eight percent of managers conduct random reviews of e-mail.
- A whopping 75 percent of the participants said an employer should have the right to read anything contained in a company-owned electronic communication system.

This last figure was up 14 percent from a 1993 survey.

So, presume your e-mail and computer are not private at your office. Companies, sensitive to productivity and liability, have the right and may exercise it to monitor you and act on the results of the monitoring. To be on the safe side, have all private and confidential electronic communications take place outside your office.

And if you are a manager or oversee others in any way, be alert for two situations. In addition to individual privacy, there is proprietary information your company wants to keep from prying eyes. E-mail is an easy way to transmit information you don't want your competitors to know. Whether it is pricing strategy or a product formula, safeguard your valuable information and limit who can see it. And if your employees use your e-mail system to cause trouble, you will be held responsible.

Understanding why companies are concerned about the personal e-mail and Web surfing that happens under their roof is easy. Those activities are best confined to outside the workplace. And, since the company presumably is not concerned with personal information about you in your off-hours either, this is a logical place to draw the line for employee privacy. Still, some companies extend their reach beyond the office—into your medical records and intimate details of your personal life.

SELF-INSURED COMPANIES AND YOUR MEDICAL RECORDS

Employers fund a substantial portion of our health care. In fact, a growing trend for companies is to be self-insured. The company contracts with a party to administer the health benefits program, but the company is the principal agent. The number of Americans who have health insurance through a self-insured employer is not insignificant. In 1993, just over 60 million individuals were covered in this manner.

Even companies that do not self-insure often provide extended health services. Employee assistance plans and on-site clinics and nurses are enhancements granted by employers for their workers and employees. In all such programs, you should expect firewalls and clear separations to protect personal medical information from supervisors or executives who can make hiring and firing decisions based on them. But this is not always the case.

Dr. David R. Linowes, a University of Illinois public policy professor, examined this issue as part of his workplace privacy studies. In 1996, he surveyed Fortune 500 companies to see whether medical information was clearly separated and protected in the big companies. One-third of the 84 respondents said they used medical records to make employment-related decisions. Linowes concluded that "The thrust is that employers don't hesitate to use this information. It's something that enters the equation concerning their investment in personnel."[25]

Southeastern Pennsylvania Transit Authority in Philadelphia is the site of a specific example of this phenomena. The Transit Authority paid Rite

Aid Pharmacy to provide medications to their workers in exchange for a breakdown on who was using what drugs. The breakdown indicated one of the employees was using AIDS medicine. The company's executives and the employee's supervisor were informed. The employee sued for loss of privacy but lost. According to the judge hearing the case, the company had a legitimate reason to delve into his records.

Corporal Joseph Vlacovsky's and Lance Corporal John Mayfield's suit against the U.S. Marine Corp had a slightly more sympathetic outcome. They refused to submit blood and tissue samples for DNA identification. The Pentagon had ordered the DNA tests, it said, only for identification purposes in case of wartime death. The two Marines feared the results would someday be used against them when they wanted civilian jobs or insurance. They were court-martialed in 1996 for refusing to take the tests and found guilty, but both obtained honorable discharges.[26]

Genetic tests and AIDS medications are susceptible to employer concerns. So are mental health problems. Dr. Steven Kenny Hoge, a spokesman for the American Psychiatry Association and practicing psychiatrist, told of his experiences in this arena. He explained that one of his jobs is to help his patients limit the disclosure in such a way that it does not intrude any more than necessary on their privacy. But Dr. Hoge states that it is not uncommon in his experience for a psychiatric patient to say: *"My employer wants all the records of my hospitalization before I can go back to work."* Dr. Hoge prefers to use another approach.

He explained, "You would write a more limited letter. That Mr. Jones came and had such and such condition and now he has been treated and he does not need (or will need) ongoing psychiatric care, but he is ready to return to work. You do not need to give the records about how Mr. Jones was manic and naked and running in the streets and doing all sorts of things that are only going to embarrass him to his employer."

Workers fret over whether the details of their medical history will adversely affect them in the workplace. Being passed by for promotion or even fired are possible outcomes of having diseases discussed and treated in what was once the privacy of a doctor's office. But other factors could also threaten your career.

PERSONAL BUT NOT PRIVATE

Senior Chief Petty Officer Timothy R. McVeigh (no relation to the man convicted of bombing the Oklahoma City federal building) was to be discharged from the Navy based on his AOL profile. The discharge was to happen even though he was a highly decorated seventeen-year Navy veteran. The sailor, based in Pearl Harbor, was out at sea in a nuclear submarine, the U.S.S. *Chicago.* On September 2, Ms. Helen Hajne, a civilian Navy volunteer, received an e-mail message through AOL regarding the toy-drive she was coordinating for the Chicago's crew members' children. The message stated that it came from the alias "boysrch," but the text of the e-mail was signed by "Tim." Unsure who the sender was, she checked the AOL profile.

The profile's name was Tim from Honolulu. Under marital status, "gay" was listed and "boy watching" was listed as one of his hobbies. It did not include any further identifying information such as full name, address, or phone number. Ms. Hajne forwarded the e-mail and directory profile to her husband, who, like McVeigh, was also a noncommissioned officer aboard the U.S.S. *Chicago.* The material found its way to the ship's captain.

At this point the matter was turned over to the Judge Advocate General's (JAG) Corp to investigate, and Lieutenant Karin Morean was put in charge. The Navy suspected the "Tim" who authored the e-mail might be Senior Chief Timothy McVeigh. The Navy felt this was a violation of the four-year-old "Don't Ask, Don't Tell, Don't Pursue" policy. Before Morean spoke with McVeigh, and without a warrant or court order, she asked a Navy paralegal, Legalman First Class Joseph Kaiser, to call AOL to verify that the account belonged to McVeigh. When Kaiser contacted AOL, he did not identify himself as a Navy investigator. But he was successful in finding out from an AOL technician that the account was indeed McVeigh's.

In providing this information, AOL violated federal law, the Electronic Communications Privacy Act. This federal law requires that government officials obtain such information from private companies only with a subpoena. They also violated their own company policy, which was to give account information only to the actual subscriber. The policy even requires verification with the last four digits of a credit card.

The Navy felt that McVeigh's AOL profile was a clear violation of the "Don't Tell" policy. A three-member naval administrative board recommended last November that McVeigh be discharged honorably based on his "homosexual statement." But on January 26, 1998, a federal judge blocked the move. U.S. District Judge Stanley Sporkin said the Navy had violated the Pentagon guidelines for investigating suspected homosexuals and had violated federal statutes meant to protect the privacy of electronic Internet users.

In Sporkin's 15-page ruling, he stated that McVeigh "did not openly express his homosexuality in a way that compromised the Pentagon's policy. Suggestions of sexual orientation in a private anonymous e-mail account did not give the Navy a sufficient reason to investigate to determine whether to commence discharge proceedings. In its actions, the Navy violated its own regulations," the judge concluded.[27]

The courts in this case upheld the privacy rights of the individual outside the workplace. From the serious matters to the silly, life outside the office is protected from your employer as long as it does not affect your ability to carry out your duties. An elected official who participates in an "I lick toes" bulletin board or a corporate officer who joins in a chat room discussion about aliens living next door are safe from their employers' reach.

Privacy at work has some clearly defined elements. Your e-mail and Web surfing are not private. The rationale is justified and understandable. You are, after all, using company time and company resources. But medical records and personal activities do not fall into this precise rationale. And both, when violated, can cause disappointment and disaster to individual privacy.

SHOPPING AND SOCIALIZING

The Internet brings into your home treasures and treats for your shopping enjoyment. When you are caught at home with a sick child, for instance, you are not limited to your stock of catalogues; you can shop anywhere in the world—and find competitive prices, too. You can spark up your social life in chat rooms by talking with people doing interesting things and debating lively topics. But each area—shopping and socializing—has privacy problems that should be explored. While shopping, you are subject to credit card theft and worse: identity theft. Socializing could bring individuals into contact with stalkers and abusers. The good news is that prudent practices can reduce your risks.

ELECTRONIC SHOPPING IS FUN

In November 1997, the Travel Industry Association of America estimated that 13.8 million Americans had used the Internet to plan their travel—with a particular emphasis on airline tickets. For 1997, online travel sales are estimated to have reached $816 million. By the year 2000, online travel sales could reach $5 billion, or close to 7 percent of U.S. airline revenues for passenger air travel. This high acceptance of the Internet is being experienced in other service products as well, such as magazines and news broadcasts. Ninety percent of Web users go online for news. There are 2,700 newspapers online and all but three of the top 50 U.S. magazines have a Web presence. Lately, shopping on the Internet has even extended to tangible goods and offers an alternative to crowded shopping malls.

Imagine being able to shop in a place where your choices are plentiful and you'll encounter no line at the cash register. The Internet offers this and more. It has stores created just for the World Wide Web such as the bookstore Amazon.com. While the largest bookstore in the physical world carries about 150,000 different books, on the Web readers can choose from 2.5 million books. This extensive choice in titles accounts for Amazon's growth in sales from $16 million in 1996 to $148 million in 1997. Barnes and Noble, the book megastore chain, launched its own online bookstore in 1997 to compete with Amazon for this rapidly growing online market.

You'll find cyber malls like CyberTown by the dozen. A cyber mall is a site on the Internet with shops, shopping services, and sometimes entertainment. And they are all open 24 hours a day. This is a feature that shoppers appreciate and use. AOL found 40 percent of their members shopped between 10 at night and 10 in the morning when regular stores are closed. These shoppers were viewing merchandise from the comfort of their homes—maybe even in their pajamas.

Retailers are certainly trying to attract shoppers to their Web stores. Many sites have snazzy virtual storefronts with sound and video clips and service departments with suggestions for the ideal present. During holiday time, some used the festive season to introduce more glitter to their sites or a warm friendly feeling by offering Christmas cookie recipes. These efforts have succeeded in bringing more visitors to the sites and more of the visitors are buying merchandise.

Barnes and Noble and the Gap both participate in the AOL electronic mall. During December 1997, they rang up $150 million in Internet sales, double their 1996 Internet sales. In total, during November and December of 1997, according to Jupitor Communications Co., a New York market research firm, online sales reached $1.1 billion. This was triple the online holiday sales of the year before. But even at $1.1 billion, it is a very small slice—only 4 percent—of total holiday shopping, which is over $50 billion.

The growing numbers of online shoppers are satisfied with their shopping experiences. This is especially true of those who are comparison shoppers. Although the technique is the same, the Internet can speed up the process. A *Forbes* reporter demonstrated this as he searched for a kitchen stove. Specifically, he wanted a Viking VGRC605 range. He called six retailers in Manhattan, several of whom weren't friendly and refused to provide a price over the phone. He finally did get a price quote. Then he went on the Web and visited the Viking Range Corporation site, on which he found the distributor list and checked with many of the listed distributors. He found a price, which included delivery, that was considerably lower than his telephone hunt had uncovered.[28]

Choice is dramatically increased online as is convenience and ease of research. There are good prices too. Virtual stores report lower operating costs than their physical counterparts. They don't have to deal with the costs of the actual store, depreciation, labor, utilities, or other expenses. But online consumers do give up their privacy.

In a physical store, you take your purchase with you when you leave. Online, you provide your name and address. This information can be coupled with click-stream data and survey information to tell the store manager more about you. While this could result in personalized service, it should be accomplished with your knowledge and permission.

CREDIT CARD THEFT AND FRAUD

Such positive attributes of Internet shopping must be considered; so must the risks. Online crooks want to capture personal information about you, including your credit card numbers, while you shop. This often happens in conjunction with another form of Internet fraud.

If You Liked Spam, You'll Like This

Internet fraud is the Web site equivalent of spam in e-mail. Like spammers, these Web sites are blatant frauds to steal visitors' money. But spam is fairly transparent, while some of these Web sites are professionally designed and written. At first glance they appear to be legitimate. But their topics track those of spam; this is the first giveaway. Figure 4.2 lists the subject categories and reflects the relative frequency of fraud report types coming into the National Consumer's League and their new program, Internet Fraud Watch.

"Consumers lose between $10 to $10,000 in Internet scams," said National Consumer League President Linda Golodner. "Cyber crooks are in your wallet with a click of the mouse." But as with spam, when you read the Web site offerings, you will usually find it clear that these are not places to put your money. The claims are always too good to be true. Extravagant promises of profits, guarantees of credit regardless of bad credit history, and incredibly low prices are examples of too good claims. Hype words like "hot" often appear, and so do testimonials. In fact, when you have to scroll through screens of testimonials and promises on many of the sites, you are still left unclear what the actual product is.

	1996	1997 (January–July)
1.	Pyramid Schemes/ Multilevel Marketing	Sale of Internet Services
2.	Business Opportunities	Sale of General Merchandise
3.	Sales of Computer Equipment/Software	Auctions
4.	Sale of Internet Services	Pyramid Schemes/ Multilevel Marketing
5.	Work-at-Home Schemes	Business Opportunities
6.	Club Memberships/ Buyers Clubs	Work-at-Home Schemes
7.	Magazine Subscriptions	Prizes and Sweepstakes
8.	Investments	Credit Card Offers
9.	Scholarly Services	Book Sales
10.	Prizes and Sweepstakes	Magazine Subscriptions

FIG. 4.2:

Top 10 Internet Scams

Source: Internet Fraud Watch

These scams and their peddlers are not much different from frauds in the physical world, but use of the Internet lends them credibility. Fortuna Alliance L.L.C., for example, has used an old investment fraud scheme—basically an unlawful pyramid sales scheme. The company induced consumers to invest in its scheme mostly by direct, person-to-person contact. But it also used its Web site, and clone sites of hundreds of members, to promote the scheme throughout the world. Potential investors were attracted to the sites. The Web site also facilitated communications between Fortuna and its widely scattered team leaders. Fortuna could not have achieved widespread success as quickly as it did without the Internet. The Federal Trade Commission filed suit against Fortuna in 1996—but not before the company had taken in an estimated $13 million from over 25,000 consumers—about half outside the U.S.—in only six months.[29]

Fortuna and others want to cheat people out of their money. But some companies or individuals want more. They operate Web sites that are looking for cash or checks and credit card numbers. They masquerade as legitimate organizations selling products. Eastern Avionics International was planning to launch its first Web site. In doing a Web search, the president, James Kantor, found his company already had a site up and operating. Kantor called the group designing his site and confirmed work was not complete and the site they were working on was not on the Web. What was going on?

The fake site Kantor found was using his catalogue. The site listed his company's merchandise and products with the same prices shown in his catalogue. The only differences were that if you ordered from this Web site, you would be giving your credit card number to crooks and receiving no merchandise. The FBI was contacted and the site was closed down. The FBI investigation found not only the fake Eastern Avionics site but 35 other fake sites launched to steal credit card numbers—not to engage in product sales. The FBI's move stopped the fake site before any customers complained to Kantor about fraud.[30]

A more serious worry—identity theft—does not appear to be increasing on the Internet. Identity theft goes beyond a criminal charging things to your credit card. It can extend to the criminal creating a complete financial life with loans, new credit cards, and mortgages all taken out in your name. In the future, the relatively easy access to personal information may change the situation. But for now, people are more vulnerable in the physical world than in cyberspace.

Federal agencies and state and local law enforcement officials are beginning to be proactive in their investigation of Internet problems. "Internet Pyramid Surf Day" is an example of this. On one day in December 1996, four federal agencies and 70 state and local law enforcement officials from 24 states notified more than 500 Internet Web sites that they may be promoting illegal pyramid schemes in violation of federal and state laws. Continued monitoring like this could stop or slow down incipient fraud before it spreads.

PROTECTING YOURSELF FROM INTERNET FRAUD

Being aware of the dangers and recognizing them is an excellent start. Good habits and practices can help, too. The Internet Fraud Watch Web site has two pages of basic Internet tips for your review (www.fraud.org/

internt/inttip/basint.htm). Here are four main habits to incorporate into your Web shopping repertoire:

- Don't judge reliability by how nice or professional a Web site may seem. Creating a Web site is relatively easy and inexpensive; anyone can do it.
- Read the text. If claims seem too wonderful, ask for more information. A legitimate company will be glad to answer; a fraudulent marketer may not.
- Do business with companies you know and trust. Be sure you know the company's reputation and where it is physically located so you can resolve problems should they arise.
- Be careful to whom you give your financial or other personal information. Con artists may try to obtain your bank account numbers, credit card numbers, Social Security number, or other personal information. Make sure you know the company is legitimate and the information is necessary for the transaction.

When using a credit card on the Web, check your Web browser. If you have a current version of Netscape Navigator or Microsoft Internet Explorer, the most popular browsers, you are in good shape. Both use what is called Secure Socket Layer (SSL) technology. On Netscape you will see a solid key icon, and on Microsoft there will be a padlock icon if your version has SSL. This technology scrambles or encrypts the purchase information. If it is intercepted by a hacker or crook, it will be unreadable. If you do not see evidence of an encryption system, you may feel more comfortable looking for the 800 number and using this instead.

Be careful, but don't be frightened. The widespread impression that giving your credit card number over the Internet makes you highly vulnerable to fraud or theft is no longer true. Though no credit card transaction is entirely secure, industry analysts are quick to point out that the risk of fraud on the Internet is no higher than when you give your credit card number over the phone or hand your card to a salesclerk. And if your credit card number is stolen, both VISA and Mastercard offer you the same protection for online transactions as for other credit card fraud. The consumer is liable for only $50.

Other technologies and systems are being devised to make consumers even more secure and private in their shopping. When Sears and Roebuck first introduced their catalogue, it revolutionized the way business was done. Isolated agrarian Americans had never before been able to purchase quality merchandise by mail. People were ready to buy necessities and save their nickels and quarters for those special items, but they were worried about sending cash through the mail. Stimulated by the mail-order business, banks began issuing money orders. There are solutions to all new business challenges.

WHEN WEBCHAT BECOMES WEBCHILL

Sandy had not been out on a date in two years. Raising her seven-year-old daughter and meeting the demands of her job as a legal secretary hadn't left her time to meet anyone who interested her. A friend told her about chat rooms and online dating. The friend had met a number of men and now had an active and fun social life. So, late one evening, Sandy logged on to a local chat room. After her initial shyness passed, she was drawn into conversations with several men. When she logged off three hours later, she silently thanked her friend for the tip. The Internet was just the place to meet great guys.

And it's also a great place to meet annoying and even dangerous guys. With growing numbers of people participating in online chat, problems with harassment and stalking are beginning to crop up. These are not only irritating sporadic e-mail messages; they can involve methodical and persistent communication that is not only deliberate, but is often angry and inappropriately sexual.

HARASSMENT IS?

Harassment can include any of these activities:

- Unwanted/unsolicited e-mail
- Unwanted/unsolicited talk requests

- Disturbing messages bulletin boards/newsgroups
- Unsolicited communications about you to coworkers, friends, and acquaintances
- Offline communication like paper mail or phone calls[31]

Jayne Hitchcock's story is an alarming one. She submitted a book proposal to a literary agency, Woodside Literary Agency, that had advertised on the Web. A representative responded to her proposal promptly and with enthusiasm, but asked for a $75 reading fee. Hitchcock balked and asked for her proposal back. She checked with a writing newsgroup on Usenet to see if others had had experience with Woodside. The experiences she heard about were not positive—several writers had paid the reading fee plus additional charges and had gotten nothing in return.

Hitchcock and other members of the writing group, misc.writing, alerted others in Usenet about their concerns. Not long afterward, she became the victim of harassment. It started with e-mail bombing; she would get 100–200 e-mails an hour. The same thing happened to her agent and several other friends. This was followed by a posting in newsgroups. In essence, the posting said, "Subject: LOVE BITES. Female International Author . . . invites you to write or call to exchange exciting fantasies with her which will be the topic of her next book."[32] This message included her phone number and address and went to more than 100 sex-related newsgroups.

Although she contacted the police and the FBI, they could do nothing to help her because she had not been directly threatened. After a little detective work, she tracked down the people she believed responsible and filed an aggravated harassment suit. This was followed by a suit filed by the New York state attorney general's office.

Lori Powell's experience had some of the same elements but was much more personal in its threats. In 1992, she started participating in a Prodigy bulletin board on child raising. Someone with whom she had never directly communicated, not one single e-mail, started sending messages to the bulletin board for everyone to see that made crude sexual suggestions about her. The problem escalated when he coupled the crude remarks with her home address in his postings. This saga continued for four years until he was sent to prison on other charges.[33]

PROTECTING YOURSELF IN A CHAT ROOM

These are cautionary tales. Internet meetings produce happy endings far more often than horror stories. This can be true for you if you follow three sensible rules for chatting carefully.

- *Be careful to whom you talk.* You don't have to get into a conversation with everyone who demands your attention. If someone makes you uncomfortable, you have the right to stop talking to him or her, no matter what your reason. Thousands of nice people are waiting out there; move on to one of them.
- *Be careful what you say.* Remember how easy it is to get a telephone number, address, and map to your house. Even if you are getting along famously with someone, keep key bits of personal information to yourself.
- *Be careful when you venture into the physical world.* Protocol on the Net requires the man to give the woman his phone number. From there, plan to meet in a well-lit public place, and tell someone where you are going, just in case.

The Internet can enlarge and better your life at work, at home, and at play; but care and prudence are the keys to avoiding unfortunate or dangerous problems. Medical information is a bigger problem. Health information moves easily, thanks to electronic transmission and computerized records; but this data does not always move to people or organizations concerned about treating disease. Is the trust between patient and doctor gone in the Electronic Age?

5

YOUR MEDICAL RECORDS: HEALING OR REVEALING?

Most Americans mistakenly assume their medical records are private. The ease with which the doctor transmits your electronic file to the expert or specialist can be dangerous when others outside the treatment arena are involved. This chapter examines the many groups interested in seeing the details of your medical history and record, why they have access, and which cases present reason for concern. A few actions you can take to prevent widespread distribution are pointed out, but this situation calls for more than just good practices. Legislative action or federal regulation is needed; therefore, the chapter ends with the proposals to safeguard your medical information.

The Internet offers excellent health information to enlighten visitors about ailments, chronic conditions, and medications. The federal government's National Institutes of Health (www.nih.gov), for instance, provides helpful tips about diet and exercise, research advances in heart disease and cancer, and even experimental research trials looking for participants.

The Electronic Age does more than provide you with medical information; it can make your visits to the doctor's office much more productive.

Envision walking in for your routine appointment. The doctor goes to his or her terminal and pulls up your file. Immediately, the first screen shows your last visit, the symptoms you suffered, and the treatment suggested. The doctor follows up on this and then moves to your examination. All measurements and test results are entered directly into the terminal. After taking your vital signs and assessing your health, the doctor prints out the results, including your blood pressure readings for the past two years, then makes suggestions for increased exercise and dietary changes and hands the printout to you.

The computerized medical system has made your visit more worthwhile for both you and the doctor; you can now leave with more information than you have ever been able to obtain. Let's go a step further. Maybe the doctor suspects a serious problem so he or she electronically sends these findings to a specialist. The specialist reviews the material and transmits suggestions for treatment back over the Internet. The ability to reach experts and provide them with the information they need to help in diagnosis and treatment of your ailment is nearly instantaneous, thanks to electronic networks.

YOUR HEALTH— IS IT EVERYONE'S BUSINESS?

Medical records, the formal story of your health, follow financial information as a very sensitive concrete privacy concern. Your personal medical information is not available on the World Wide Web. It is, however, being collected and circulated on private electronic networks that weave in and out through the Internet. Medicine, like so many other disciplines, has entered the Electronic Age, taking advantage of the storage and analytical ability of computers and the speed and convenience of electronic networks.

Over $10 billion are spent annually to bring paper records into the Electronic Age. Health organizations are beginning to develop new means of protecting health information as it is put online. Most health organizations, however, have developed policies and practices in an ad hoc fashion, reacting to individual incidents rather than setting a general policy. This was one of the insights from the National Research Council's Committee on Maintaining Privacy and Security in Health Care Applications of the National Information Infrastructure during a series of site visits in 1997 to six organizations that collect, process, and store electronic medical records. The six sites were selected based on solid reputations in electronic record development, but the committee found most had no formal policies, training, or review—these were the leadership sites!

A surprising number of organizations, including care providers, insurers, state public health organizations—sometimes even employers, drug manufacturers, and law enforcement agencies—receive information about you.

If it isn't already, your medical record will soon be an Electronic Medical Record (EMR) and even easier to circulate.

An EMR will have many clear benefits for you. For example, it will be easy to move. If your doctor wants to consult a specialist hundreds of miles away, he or she can electronically send your record and within minutes be able to discuss the diagnosis or treatment possibilities with the specialist.

Since the record is simple to move from one place to another, people treating you will not have to ask you the same questions you have already answered because the answers are clearly stated in your EMR. Reducing redundant queries and improving access to care are among the benefits you can expect. And frankly, there is no visible evidence that this is dangerous. The statistics on electronic medical information being pirated are not growing. Occasional anecdotes, several of which are troublesome, come forward; but no red or yellow lights are flashing at this time.

Having said that, let's remember one other thing. This is a new medium and a new application. The time to anticipate problems and vulnerabilities is during its nascent period. This is also the time to consider how we want our medical information to be handled. This technological approach to medicine occurs at a time of upheaval in the health-care industry. No longer is a family doctor present at your birth and there to treat you throughout your life. You now deal with a family of health-care professionals and payment systems, all of which need or want access to your medical records.

YOUR TREATMENT CONFIDANT

Your personal physician is the guardian of your medical privacy. Knowing he or she will keep your secrets and embarrassing stories confidential is an important part of your relationship. This trust creates the environment in which you can frankly reveal your health problems. It stems from a tradition of confidentiality beginning with the Greeks and the Hippocratic Oath, which states: ". . . and whatsoever I shall see or hear in the course of my profession, as well as outside my profession in my intercourse with men, if it be what should not be published abroad, I will never divulge holding such things to be holy secret." This is the oath to which the Greek physician, regarded as Father Medicine, adhered. Doctors have adopted this standard as a professional ethic and strive to uphold it.

Since they are intimately involved in your treatment and significant contributors to your record, there is no question that personal physicians should have access to your record. And so should you. Yet patients rarely see their own records. They may not know to ask for it or may have been discouraged from asking by their health plans, insurers, and even health-care providers. In addition, the right to see one's own medical records is not a guaranteed right. Only 28 states have any legislation that mandates access to medical data, and even this is spotty. For example, the District of Columbia's mandate is for mental health records only. Mandates in some other states refer only to hospital records or only to personal physician data.

Extended treatment teams include consulting physicians and specialists, clinical laboratories, and your local hospital. As with your primary doctor, the consulting physician/specialist assesses your medical needs and develops an appropriate treatment plan. This is then documented as part of your record. Either the specialist or your primary doctor can prescribe diagnostic tests. These tests, whether a mammogram or a blood sample, also become part of your record. The local hospital provides care for you as directed by your primary doctor. They'll provide a record of services and treatment. Donna Ganzer with Community Concerns on Information Security gave a presentation in March of 1996, in which she estimated that as many as 400 people may see part or all of your medical record during a hospital stay!

To be effective, your treatment team needs access to your information but must respect its value to you and not treat it in a cavalier manner. The National Research Council (NRC) conducted a study in 1997 on electronic health information. Their methodology included gathering a mixed study team of established, knowledgeable professionals to evaluate the risks related to electronic health information and to make recommendations to mitigate or ameliorate them. Half the study team worked in the medical profession as physicians or medical administrators. The other half was comprised of experts in computer security and electronic information systems. When the team members journeyed to their visits to six health-care sites, the computer security and electronic information experts were surprised at how little attention was paid to security and privacy. Even when the computer systems were carefully planned to ensure privacy, the electronic experts were frightened by the way anyone could walk in or out of the facility. One team member likened it to having the back door shut tight while the front door was wide open.

PAYMENT INFORMATION

Those who provide our treatment have a sound reason to see our complete medical record. What about those involved in payment? Some certainly have reason to know about your treatment, but exactly who in the payment process should see your record and how much of it should they see? Your first opportunity to consider these issues is when you select health benefit plans. When choosing between health maintenance organizations, preferred provider organizations, and conventional indemnity insurance, you are given information about services and rates, but not about how the organization handles personal information. The program descriptions do not outline the way your health records will be stored and controlled.

Even if these policies were detailed, it might not matter to you. Fundamentally, most of us give away our right to control our personal information when we consent to allowing dissemination of our information. When you go for care, whether to your primary provider, a hospital, or other medical facility, you're asked to sign a waiver for the release of your medical records. Even if you have no memory of doing this, you probably did. Usually you are asked to sign a blanket waiver that may say, for example: "I authorize any physician, hospital, or other medical provider to release to (insurer) any information regarding my medical history, symptoms, treatment, exam results, or diagnosis."

This consent gives the health benefit companies and health insurers carte blanche access to your records if the treatment team cooperates. Health insurers appreciate unlimited access to your files so they can not only contribute to your health but can also run an effective organization and control costs. Employers and insurers have all been working toward reducing the spiraling medical costs. Understanding your treatment helps them curb expenditures. The question is: How much do insurers need to know?

In the past, health benefit companies did not obtain your complete record. Rather, they viewed a greatly abbreviated form that provided enough information to categorize the disease and treatment. To satisfy their desire to control costs, insurance companies want more, and the medical profession is very uncomfortable. In February of 1997, the National Committee on Vital and Health Statistics held a subcommittee meeting on privacy and confidentiality. Dr. Donald Palmisano spoke for the American Medical Association, summing up his and AMA's view: "But the evolution of electronic medical data has intensified our existing concerns about access to and now even commerce in patients' confidential medical information. . . . The growing number of third parties demanding information has eroded patients' security that the information shared with their doctor is going to help in their individual case."[34]

Palmisano's colleague, Dr. Steven Kenny Hoge, speaking for the American Psychiatry Association, agreed: "Medical information has increasingly been put to uses that are not intended to serve patient interest in any way. Third-party demands for access have increased with attendant risks to invasions of privacy. Electronic storage of medical information raises serious privacy concerns since these systems by design facilitate access, transmission, and duplication of medical records."[35]

Dr. Hoge's concern extends to the entire arena of mental health care. Health insurers are engaging in active review of this area. In an article for the *Washington Post Magazine,* author Arthur Allen interviewed dozens of psychotherapists and patients. According to the therapists, managed care companies frequently balk at reimbursing extensive therapy without exhaustive information about the ailments of the patients.[36] There was a time when your doctor decided the best treatment for you; today the doctor is no longer alone in the decision, as insurers join in.

LIMITED CHOICES TO PROTECT PRIVACY

What strategies can patients use to combat providing a detailed portrait of their medical life? The practice of paying out of pocket rather than submitting an insurance claim is a tactic used frequently by those wanting to circumvent the collection of personal information. In one survey, 11 percent of respondents—representing five million Americans—reported that they or a member of their immediate family had personally paid for a medical test, treatment, or counseling rather than submit a bill or claim under a health plan.[37]

Of course, another strategy is not to seek treatment or to provide partial information to doctors. Not getting treatment is a tricky area, particularly when genetic testing is involved. Hundreds of genetic tests are currently available, but most are not absolutely conclusive. An exception is the test for Huntington's disease, a degenerative brain disorder with a genetic link that can be traced. Some people in families with the disease have been denied insurance coverage unless they agree to undergo a genetic test and, of course, the result must be negative.

WHO KNOWS YOUR FAMILY SECRETS?

Health benefit companies and health insurance companies have arranged for companies with specialties to handle a portion of your benefit program. Pharmacy benefits and pharmaceutical benefits management companies, for example, process patients' medication claims, monitor prescription usage, and perform utilization reviews.

Your insurer will give you a card identifying you and your pharmaceutical benefits management company. You show the card at the local drugstore when you are having your prescription filled. The pharmacy will check via computer to verify your deductible. The system will detail other medications you are on so the pharmacist can be warned about problematic medication combinations. In the longer term, the company can check how often you refill to determine whether you are following your treatment schedule. This monitoring, particularly if more than one doctor is prescribing medicine, contributes to your health.

As with all the people and organizations mentioned, pharmaceutical benefits management companies have personally identifiable information about the doctors you visit, the drugs you are taking, and probably the diseases you have. Because many other companies would find this information extremely useful, it is no surprise that the two largest pharmaceutical benefits management companies are owned by major pharmaceutical manufacturers. Medco is owned by Merck and Company, and PCS Health Systems Inc. is owned by Eli Lilly and Company. When companies in this industry join, they must carefully consider the ramifications. On one hand, the combination creates a new value and strength for the corporations; on the other, the corporations have to be wary of conflicts of interest and questionable practices. In these instances, data sharing among affiliates is limited, but complex overlaps make it difficult to ensure that data is not shared inappropriately.

For example, a pharmaceutical manufacturer could hire or contract with its affiliate, a benefits manager, to identify doctors prescribing a competitor's drug. The benefits manager would be able to conduct this analysis because he or she has your specific records and the records of others. Evidence of this is illustrated by a case in which a Minnesota pharmaceutical company acquired PBM, a pharmaceutical benefits management company. PBM used information in its database to try to convince physicians to prescribe drugs manufactured by its parent pharmaceutical company.

This scenario can be played out with other partners. Several insurance companies have established their own provider networks. An example of this is Aetna's acquisition of U.S. Healthcare. One survey found that 15 percent of hospitals owned an HMO, up from 10 percent two years earlier.[38] As the industry consolidates and single companies expand, their reach in services and markets, benefits and efficiencies are natural. But, these companies may have access through one of their affiliates to personally identifiable information. Special caution and oversight is appropriate.

YOUR VITAL STATISTICS

The private sector, from health insurers to your own company, are also interested in the details of your medical records. For different reasons, so are state and local governments. In their public sector role, they need to track and monitor the health statistics of those living in their area. Not all data is personally identifiable, but some is. The National Research Council's book, *For the Record: Protecting Electronic Health Information,* investigated the typical health information collected by state health departments, using the state of Washington as a model. Here are just a few of the 23 data sets noted in the study:

- Hospital discharge data
- Clinic visit records
- Child immunization tracking
- AIDS reporting system
- Birth certificate file
- Cancer registries
- Death certificate file
- Sexually transmitted disease morbidity and epidemiological report
- Child abuse and neglect data

The data collected are usually aggregated, but not always. After having a baby, most new parents receive free samples or coupons from baby product companies. The companies checked with the state registries to develop their mailing list. In this case, new parents are rewarded for having their personally identifiable information in a public database.

Databases for sexually transmitted diseases need to be treated with particular care, but are not necessarily handled so. A worker in Florida's public health system downloaded onto a disk 4,000 names of individuals who tested HIV positive. He copied the disk and mailed it to all the major newspapers in Florida.

Sometimes the data are aggregated to begin with and later become personally identifiable. In Louisiana, physicians are obligated to report that a patient has a venereal disease and confirm that the patient is undergoing treatment. A number or letter code is given to the patient and this is the information the health agency obtains. If the patient refuses to be treated or stops treatment before it is complete, the physician is obligated to attach a name to the number/letter code to the health agency so they can take action before others are contaminated. Tuberculosis cases are treated similarly.

Law enforcement and governmental investigative agencies fit under the government category as well. While officers and investigators may acknowledge the importance of medical privacy, they feel protecting such information is moot when fighting crime. Should a drug dealer wounded in a gang shootout or a bank robber sprayed in the face with dyes placed between the bills seek medical treatment? Such examples represent situations in which physical evidence can be vital to the identification of a suspect.

Successful investigation of crimes and prosecution may require confirmation of distinguishing body marks, like tattoos or scars, to identify the criminal or blood type and DNA information to link a criminal to the crime. A search warrant is required for these pieces of information. If a warrant was not properly obtained, the evidence would be excluded during a trial.

The white-collar version of robbery and killing is fraud. Figures covering the full spectrum of the health-care industry run as high as $52 billion a year. The FBI has 300 agents working specifically on health-care fraud with 2,000 pending investigations.[39] A typical case would involve a doctor or laboratory billing for services that are not medically necessary. To investigate such a case, the FBI needs identifiable medical records.

Mr. Neil Gallagher, deputy assistant director, Criminal Investigative Division of the Federal Bureau of Investigation, reviewed one such investigation before the February 1997 Subcommittee on Privacy and Confidentiality, National Committee on Vital and Health Statistics. In a single case in Louisiana, the FBI obtained 2,000 personally identifiable records. After a general review for trends and focus, the 200 best records are selected for more detailed review. By and large, they use the grand jury or administrative subpoena process for these investigations. At any time, your medical record could become part of an investigation like this one.

The same subpoena process is used in malpractice cases. A lawyer in a malpractice case can request medical records similar to the case in which he or she is involved. The medical community is bound to provide these records. Some medical practices make a point of removing the patient's name from the medical record before turning it over to the lawyer, but this is not a universal policy.

TOO MANY PEOPLE KNOW TOO MUCH

One NRC study developed a story to illustrate all the organizations and people who could look at the medical records of a fictional character, Alice. Alice's medical records were seen by many mentioned previously, including lawyers, law enforcement personnel, doctors, insurers, and others. At the conclusion of the tale, a figure (duplicated as in figure 5.1) was provided to demonstrate the possible flow of medical record information.

With all these groups viewing medical records, patients such as Alice might be reassured if mechanisms were in place to regulate or monitor the use of their health information in such sectors as insurance, benefits management, or marketing. But few such mechanisms exist. Patients worry that they have no way of knowing what violations of privacy occur and whether they have a viable method of redress if they do discover violations. They also fear their employers will use information to which they

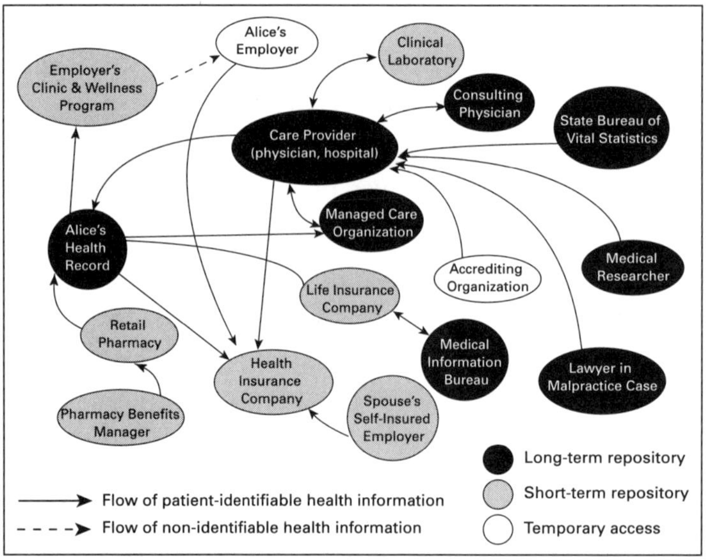

FIG. 5.1:
Flows of Alice's Health Information

Source: NRC's For the Record: Protecting Electronic Health Information

have access to deny employment or a promotion. The Department of Health and Human Services and the Congress share this concern and are taking steps to protect medical records.

A LEGISLATIVE DIAGNOSIS

In 1996, the Health Insurance Portability and Accountability Act was passed. This act makes it easier for people who are between jobs, but unemployed, to get health insurance. One section of this Act, Section 264, called for administrative simplification. The goal was to investigate uniform standards for electronic transactions in health administration. The Secretary of Health and Human Services, Donna Shalala, was tasked with studying the issue of standards in content and format and reporting her recommendations to Congress.

Secretary Shalala's team studied the literature and, through their National Committee on Vital and Health Statistics, held six days of hearings on this subject. After analyzing testimony, it was clear that they would have to make tough choices between the privacy needs of citizens and the needs of the health-care system. On September 11, 1997, Secretary Shalala presented the recommendations to the Committee on Labor and Human Resources and the Committee on Finance of the U.S. Senate, and to the Committee on Commerce and the Committee on Ways and Means of the House of Representatives. In addition to presenting her recommendations, she testified on her findings and answered the questions of the Senate Committee on Labor and Human Resources. Her opening remarks were chilling. "Let me be frank. The way we protect the privacy of our medical records right now is erratic at best—dangerous at worst."[40] After reviewing the problem, for the Congressional committees, Secretary Shalala made several recommendations.

A NEW APPROACH

While states do have medical record protection laws, they are an assortment of laws with differing priorities and coverage. There is a federal role to provide every American citizen with a floor or foundation of medical record privacy protection. The states can then build on this foundation in a way that best serves the residents of their state. The recommendations proposed by Secretary Shalala can be read at the Department of Health and Human Services (DHHS) Web site, http://aspe.os.dhhs.gov/admnsimp/pvcimles.htm. They affect health-care providers, those who pay for health care, and anyone hired by organizations that pay, including groups such as pharmaceutical benefits management companies. The recommendations are not directed toward employers (unless they are providing payment) nor workman compensation programs.

The recommendations change the meaning of consent form. Now, patients must sign consent forms and the forms in general provide no useful information to the patient. In the proposed system, the consent form would inform the patient what information is going to be given to others and why. The insurer or plan operator also will inform the patients how they can access their records and, if errors are discovered, the procedure for correction.

After the patient reads and signs the consent form, information can move freely for two principal reasons: treatment and payment. Information cannot move to employers for hiring, promotion, or firing purposes. But information can move for oversight, life and safety emergencies, and public health purposes. There is no change to the current system for law enforcement access or research activities.

But, the organizations in which your information is circulating are entrusted to protect it against deliberate and inadvertent misuse. For example, a provider should be able to use identifiable health information for mailing reminders to patients to schedule appointments, but should not be able to make available its patient list to a health company for use in a direct mailing announcing a new product or service.[41] Real and severe penalties are proposed for violators. These include fines and imprisonment for people obtaining health information under false pretenses or knowingly disclosing information outside proper treatment and payment circles.

WHAT HAPPENS NEXT?

Congress has until August 1999 to pass legislation to protect medical records. If it does not, DHHS is required to develop regulations. DHHS is already preparing for this possibility. In late 1998, a Notice of Proposed Rule Making will appear. This notice will review the recommendations and call for public comment. It will not include one controversial aspect of the Health Insurance Portability and Accountability Act, the creation of a unique patient identifier. A unique patient identifier would be a number each citizen in the health-care system was assigned that would easily allow the health-care system to track the care of that citizen. This sensitive topic is not part of Secretary Shalala's recommendations and will be approached cautiously.

In Congress, one bill by Senators Edward Kennedy and Patrick Leahy has been introduced (www.senate.gov/~leahy/s971028.html) and another by Senator Robert Bennett is being developed. The Bennett Bill, Medical Information Sharing Protection Act, was on the verge of release in February when an unanticipated incident occurred.

BLURRING LINES IN HEALTH INFORMATION

CVS Corporation and Giant Food, Incorporated have major pharmacy units in the Washington, D.C., area. Both entered into an agreement with Elensys, Incorporated, a company based in Massachusetts. The agreement involved CVS and Giant providing Elensys with names and addresses of their customers who had not refilled prescriptions.

Elensys, using CVS and Giant stationery, wrote to the customers to remind them to keep taking their medicine or to pitch a new product for treatment of the customers' ailments. Needless to say, Elensys was funded for this activity by pharmaceutical drug manufacturers. One such letter said: *"Our records indicate that you have tried to stop smoking using a prescription nicotine replacement product. We hope you successfully quit smoking but if you, like many others who have tried to quit, are still smoking we have good news for you."*[42] The letter goes on to tout the qualities of a new drug, ZYBAN. The letter is signed "Your CVS Pharmacists" but includes a notice in fine print that the mailing was supported by Glaxo Wellcome, Inc., maker of ZYBAN.

CVS, Giant, and Elensys argued that this was not a misuse of personal information. It was actually a technique to improve customer treatment. Customers did not agree. Two days after the story was reported in the local papers, Giant had over 75 individuals call and express their concern and anger. Customer response stopped the program. But the sale and disclosure of personal health information continues to be big business. Patient Direct Metromail recently advertised that it had 7.6 million names of people suffering from allergies, 945,000 suffering from bladder-control problems, and 558,000 suffering from yeast inflections. The blurring line between marketing and treatment must be taken into account as regulations and legislation are considered.

Harnessing the revolutions in computers and the Internet can breathe productive new life into the health-care delivery system of our citizens. But the health-care delivery system must continue to be based on trust between doctors and patients and the privacy of medical records. Citizens are limited in what they can do to engender this trust; they can make sure their voices are heard. The government, however, has a vital role to play and is prepared to recommend safeguards to health-care privacy in this ever-changing world. Next, recommendations must become reality.

Health-care privacy is another topic best handled separately. Another special issue is your children's safety on the Internet. The constantly changing world of the Internet can be an ideal playground for your children. With their intuitive grasp of all things electronic, children are at home talking with their friends in a chat room or visiting a Web site. But does the Internet harbor dangers to your children that you should worry about? Absolutely! And some of these dangers are not evident to the naked eye.

6

YOUR CHILDREN IN CYBERSPACE

At play. The phrase conjures visions of children in a green field or meadow on a bright day. They are running in circles playing hide-and-seek or darting about to a vigorous dodgeball game all the while laughing and yelling. The reality is, however, that they are just as likely to be indoors, alone, in front of a computer. They are yelling, yes, but at the characters on the screen. This chapter discusses the subtle and obvious dangers of the Internet for your children. Pornography sites abound and curious children look forward to checking them out. Some children, more vulnerable than curious, are targets for pedophiles and molesters using Internet chat rooms as their entry. It also explores marketing manipulations aimed at your children. This isn't the regulated world of television; it is a marketer's paradise and you'll see why.

A GENERATION OF WEBWATCHERS

The cyberworld is an exciting one for children. Since children are more comfortable with computers than adults, they relish their access to the Internet. The computer has the color and animation of the TV world and lets children actually interact with characters in games and on home pages, socialize with friends from around the world, and be exposed to ideas outside their everyday experiences.

Studies vary on the number of children on the Internet. FIND/SVP, an upstate New York research firm, reported in December 1997 that nearly 10 million children were active on the Internet. This is 14 percent of the total population of children in the United States. In a more conservative estimate, Jupiter Communications reports five million youth between the ages of 2 and 17 used the Internet or an online service from school or home in 1996. Regardless of the baseline number, all sources agree that the figure is growing. David Britt, chief executive of Children's Television Workshop explains: "It's not surprising . . . that many of the newest generation can click a mouse before they can tie a shoe. And that they've become just as comfortable with e-mail and with PCs as with pen and paper . . ."[43]

These growing numbers of children are spending more time on the Internet. Market research even suggests that the time online is starting to cut into time spent watching television. As parents and responsible adults, we have to evaluate this situation from the standpoint of threats and vulnerabilities of this new medium to our children. We understand television. Many of us have fond memories of Bullwinkle and Roadrunner cartoons.

It used to be that children spent Saturday mornings in the living room or family room with one of our parents walking through on a regular basis. Sure, the programs we watched had commercials, but the advertisements were clearly distinguishable from the program. The sound often increased, as did the visual intensity. In fact, sometimes we liked the commercials better than the program! But there were limits. The Federal Communication Commission (FCC) made sure the host of a program didn't try to sell products to children. Regulators recognized that the host's position as an authority figure was too powerful in the minds of his audience. To have the host pitch a product was considered excessive. The FCC also limited the amount of advertising time in children's shows.

These measures drew clear lines between advertising/marketing and content. The content improved over the years in color and detail, but TV remains one-way communication. The interaction between the children's TV programs and the child occurs in his or her imagination, not in reality.

How different the Internet is! None of the rules or traditions separating entertainment from advertising/marketing apply. And the compelling ability of children to interact with the program or people beyond what they may imagine creates a very different and potentially dangerous medium.

Where is your computer? Unlike the TV, which is typically located in a central place, the computer is more often in a room removed from family gathering areas—the spare bedroom upstairs, the study down the hall, or in the child's own room. Older children can leave the family environment to enter into their own world with their own friends in chat rooms and via e-mail. They value their online friendships. Some move from friendships to flirting and romance, establishing cybergirlfriends and cyberboyfriends long before they would be allowed to date in the offline world. Increasing numbers of young teens will have their first romance at younger ages and it will be on the Internet. They may also have their first exposure to harassment or sexually explicit conversations and pictures.

WHAT ARE PARENTS CONCERNED ABOUT?

And parents, responsible adults, and communities are concerned. Greenberg Research, a national survey and polling firm, conducted several focus groups of parents to seek their voices in this issue. In reporting to the Federal Trade Commission (FTC) during its summer 1997 hearings, Stanley Greenberg, chairman and chief executive officer of this firm, explained the response of the focus group participants. He did not find pure excitement and enthusiasm about children using the Internet.

Rather he found positive sentiments mixed with worry and anxiety. He read quotes such as the following from Chicago women who participated:

> It used to be all fun and exciting, but then when you hear about all the pornographic and stuff on there now, it's more like, oh, God, I'm going up there and I'm going to sit there with them.
>
> You think about people on the Internet they were showing how to make bombs when there was that unabomber thing. Kids don't need to know those things.[44]

Within the framework of this survey, Greenberg Research found genuine concerns from parents. These concerns centered on the problem of indecent material on the Internet and children being exposed to it. Indecent material was their first priority. Further down on a parent's list of concerns was the collecting of personal information from their children without parental permission.

Personal information collection was addressed in a quantitative manner by the Louis Harris/Alan Westin representative national survey. In a statistically valid manner, the survey showed that parents are deeply troubled by the online environment and are concerned about its intrusive and harmful nature and consequences.

The 14 million parents with children 16 years old and younger who participated in the Harris/Westin survey were questioned about the issues concerning personal information collection online. Some of their responses follow:

- Sixty-four percent said it is not acceptable to ask children to provide their e-mail names.
- Fifty-six percent said no to e-mail and more detailed information like hobbies and activities.
- Seventy-two percent said it is not acceptable to ask children to provide their real names and addresses.
- Ninety-seven percent said it is not acceptable for companies to ask names and addresses and then to rent or sell those names to others.[45]

The parents in this national survey and in the focus groups want to protect their wards. Protect from whom? The immediate answer is from predators. You want to ensure your children are free from indecent and physically terrifying situations—whether due to pornography peddlers or pedophiles. But there is a more insidious threat—Web marketers. Let's take each issue in turn.

PERDITION AND PORNOGRAPHY

Erica W. is 16 and an enthusiastic user of the America Online Buddy List. The Buddy List has the user provide AOL with a list of friends that can be notified whenever Erica is online. The friends then can send her a message if they are online, too. The message(s) pops up on Erica's screen in a form similar to e-mail. Some adults find this practice interferes with their private time. When they are online, they want to work on the task and complete it without annoying interruptions.

Young people, on the other hand, welcome the opportunity to socialize even if it intrudes on homework. Erica would either carry on separate e-mail conversations with her friends or maybe move into their chat room to continue the gossip and fun. She enjoyed her Buddy List pals and participated regularly.

At holiday time, Erica and her family visited her grandparents in Arizona. Her grandparents had just subscribed to AOL so Erica logged on. She sent messages to all her friends but got no response. So, she moved into one of the established chat rooms to interact with new teens. She started talking to a boy who was fun to chat with. They talked about where they lived, their schools, and their friends. Erica liked her new electronic friend and enjoyed his interest in her. Flattered, she responded positively when he asked if she would like a picture of him.

In just minutes she received the picture. It was of a completely naked boy with nothing left to the imagination. Wisely, she called her mother and they logged off and notified AOL. Erica wasn't looking for pornography—but in her innocence, she stumbled on it.

Had she been looking for pornography, she could have easily found it because there are over 60,000 Web sites featuring adult material. This material is not only "dirty" pictures of the *Playboy* variety; images on some sites meet the constitutional test for obscenity. They are available on free sites, sites leased by access providers like AOL, and on for-fee Web sites carried by the major access providers.

Scarier still, minors have no protection from such obscenity. On June 26, 1996, the Supreme Court struck down provisions of the Communications Decency Act that were intended to curb the proliferation of pornography on the Net. The court did so on grounds that the provisions violated free speech provisions in the U.S. Constitution. Now it's open season for pornographers, hate literature, and child molesters.

Pedophiles on the Web

Another law enforcement issue is predators. Between 1992 and 1996, the Justice Department federal court filings against those suspected of dealing in Internet child pornography increased by 162 percent. Court filings against those who transport minors with the intent to engage in criminal sexual activity grew by 263 percent.[46] Just what percentage of this increase in suspected pornography and minor transportation occurred on the Internet is not clear, but examples of such cases are numerous.

George "Junior" Budinsky, a 10-year-old, disappeared from his home in Brentwood, Maryland, in 1993. Both the FBI and the local police (Prince George's County, Maryland, detectives) identified two suspects who had sexually exploited numerous juvenile males for over a quarter of a century. Officers who delved into the activities of these suspects found that they had routinely employed computers to transmit images showing frontal nudity or sexually explicit conduct of minors.

The next case didn't even include the common practice of exchanging worldwide pornographic materials, including names and addresses of children. When officials searched the disks of a Minnesota prison inmate thought to be trafficking in child pornography over the Internet, they found an annotated list of thousands of children from small towns in Minnesota. The annotations—"latchkey kids," "cute," and "Little Ms. pageant winner"—confirmed officials' suspicions.[47]

Beyond exchanging lists, pedophiles have a number of advantages when they operate on the Internet. The sheer size of the Internet with its millions of Web sites makes it difficult for law enforcement agencies to keep track of their activities. In addition, pedophiles using the Internet often employ methods to encrypt pictures and photographs that require special technology to decode. These technologies are discussed in chapter 8.

When a pedophile or molester is on the prowl, he (and occasionally she) will frequently use the online persona of a child. Haunting the sites, chat rooms, and electronic bulletin boards young people visit, the pedophile will look for a lonely or vulnerable child. The child or teenager may be very unhappy, have few friends, feel that he or she does not fit in, or be having a difficult time with parents. Basically, the child is longing for attention. The pedophile or molester begins developing a relationship. This relationship can occur at the start in public chat rooms. Pedophiles may portray themselves as much younger than they are. Several cases involve older men who said they were in their 20s targeting young teenage females. Fortunately in one particular case, a female target turned out to be an undercover agent.

Another technique is for the pedophile/molester to switch roles. A child is online in a chat room. The pedophile/molester representing himself as a child is there too. At some point after he has established a relationship with the child, the pedophile/molester will suggest a meeting with a friend, an older friend, who really wants to meet the child. The pedophile/molester posing as the child then changes persona and goes online with the child, this time as an older friend.

In direct, one-on-one communication by e-mail or in chat rooms, the pedophile/molester demonstrates that he is an interested friend wanting to know about the child, identifying with the child's problems because they are similar to the pedophile/molester's. As trust increases, the pedophile will try to break down the child's inhibitions. This can be as blatant as showing the child sexual pictures or as subtle as positive reinforcement and understanding. Making the child feel special and loved in a way no one else can is the prelude to an encounter, a sexual encounter, with the child. These tactics work. A computer consultant from Rockville, Maryland, contacted over 100 young girls online before an FBI task force stopped him.

HOW YOU CAN PROTECT YOUR CHILDREN

Remember when your parents told you not to talk to strangers and not to accept any gifts, candy, or puppies from people you didn't know? This guidance needs to be expanded to include strangers and dangers on the Internet. Just as your parents occasionally questioned and reminded you, so too must you question and remind your children. Several organizations offer tips for keeping your children safe that are listed in the resource section. Review them and the ideas presented here; then tailor them to fit your children and your parenting style. You can use these tips as a starting point:

1. Don't use the Internet without permission.
2. Adhere to time limits for surfing and chatting.
3. Don't exchange pictures or photos with anyone.
4. Don't give your name, phone number, e-mail address, where you live, or the name of your school to strangers.
5. Choose a code name and make sure it doesn't reveal too much (if your name is Nancy and you are 14, "Nancy14" would be a poor choice of code name).
6. If you are uncomfortable, get out and tell your parents.
7. Do not arrange meetings in the real world without your parents' permission.

The harm in pornography is obvious. Another less blatant harm that not all parents agree is a cause for worry is that marketers are targeting their children. Some may not even be aware that this is happening. Companies big and small have a growing interest in children as customers or targets. After all, children's direct buying power has grown. In a single year, teenagers will spend $67 billion while children under 12 will spend $14 billion.[48]

KIDDIE SITES AND BIG BUCKS

Companies are eager for children to buy their products. Advertising and marketing are the means to entice children, and where better to advertise and market than on the Internet—the place with no regulatory safeguards and a growing target audience. Companies develop computer environments that are rich in color and motion. Children enter these environments when they visit the Web sites and find themselves in a world of brand loyalty–building, all the while believing they are playing a game. Or they will explore a Web site where they inadvertently answer questions and provide information a company will use to build a one-on-one relationship with them and, in addition, may even sell the data they gather to other companies.

Commerce is the American way, but drawing limits to protect children is certainly appropriate. The techniques companies use to capture our children's attention are becoming more sophisticated. Companies that sell toys, snack food, games, electronic magazines (e-zines), accessories, and clothing are launching sites with your child in mind. But your child's spending money is not the only thing these companies are interested in. Your child can be the company's entry point into your family's private affairs.

The sophisticated techniques companies are using on the Web are aimed at personal data collection and relationship establishment. The Consumer Federation of America (CFA) and Center for Media Education (CME) detailed these techniques in the book *Web of Deception*, published in 1996. This work was updated when CME's Shelley Pasnik, CME Director of Children's Policy, and Kathryn Montgomery, President of CME, spoke before the FTC in the summer of 1997 about online privacy concerns for children.

The examples Pasnik and Montgomery used, although such techniques may not still be practiced by some companies, provide a picture of how

Web sites advertise to children and the techniques Web site operators use to learn about your child and your family. Of the 38 sites CME reviewed, 90 percent actively collected personally identifiable information.

Getting to You Through Your Children

In chapter 3 we talked about technologies the Web site operator can use to collect information without the visitor's knowledge. Click-stream data lets online advertisers know where visitors go and how long they stay. This is usually aggregated information, but one specific technique—the use of cookies—not only tracks visitor/user movements; it stores the information on the visitor's hard drive so the site will recognize the visitor if he or she returns. This all goes on quietly and invisibly. Neither adults nor children can see what is happening.

This information alone has some value to companies for marketing, but becomes a gold mine when married to detailed personal profiles. That is why many sites will ask questions or survey the children who visit. And they have every confidence that children will answer, and answer correctly.

When adults are faced with an online questionnaire or survey, they review their options. One option is to simply not answer; another is to respond; but a third option is to lie. The Georgia Tech GVU 6th WWW User Survey found that this third option is commonly used by adults. Adults falsify their registration at Web sites with some regularity. They do so for a number of reasons. The reason mentioned most frequently was that they didn't know how the information was going to be used and consequently felt uncomfortable or distrustful of the situation.

Children don't assess their options in the same manner; in fact, few probably even think about direct lying. But if companies are savvy, they create an environment where children want to tell them about themselves. One way is by making the child want to belong. At the FTC hearing, Pasnik pointed out the Glossy Girl site (www.glossy.com). This site preyed on the desire to belong. It talked about how cool Glossy Girls were and how they wanted the visitor to come and gossip with them. This stage-setting approach lets the company ask the visitor questions. The 20 questions requested personal information, such as name and e-mail address, but also preferences in computers, magazines, and other areas. The questions were hip in their presentation, not the same old boring ones often encountered. "The hills are alive with the sound of music—what are your favorite songs?" was the approach. This appeals to the market target (teenage and preteen girls) and results in higher participation.

Sometimes the survey or questions do not appear all at one time. The visitor may answer some personal information at the beginning of the site (name and e-mail address) and then move deeper into the site, where he or she will be asked additional questions about preferences, hobbies, and habits. Nickelodeon, for example, coupled the survey with another effective technique to obtain participation. Developers of this site offered a sweepstakes prize of a big-screen TV. To register for the drawing, visitors were asked questions about their pets and the sports they liked to play and watch, and their interest in drawing or painting.

Using incentives works for companies. In this survey, it was used 40 percent of the time, presented in different flavors. Sometimes it was a sweepstakes to enter, as in the Nickelodeon case. Other times, free stuff—candy, screen savers, or merchandise—is offered. Children like the idea of winning and are prone to reveal personal information in exchange—even when the incentive is as simple as the chance to win one of the 500 samples of jelly beans the Jelly Belly (www.jellybelly.com) site offered in exchange for personal information.

Good and Bad Privacy Policies

The information Jelly Belly receives could help develop new marketing campaigns and products because it now knows more about your child. Or the information could be sold to other companies seeking the same goal. The site was frank about this aspect. At the bottom of its home page was a link that read, "Here's more legal stuff." After clicking on this, a screen with the *Top Ten Rules for Cybersurfers* came up. One of the rules stated:

> If you don't want the world to know something, don't post it on the site in any survey, form, bulletin board, or anyplace else. That's because anything you disclose to us is ours. That's right—ours. So we can do anything we want with the stuff you post. We can reproduce it, disclose it, transmit it, publish it, broadcast it, and post it someplace else. We can even send it to your mother (as soon as we find her address). Not only that, we can even use any ideas, concepts, know-hows, or techniques you post any way we want to, including developing, manufacturing, and marketing products, or other stuff using the information you post.[49]

Actually, this is brutal, not just frank. It's one thing to be nonchalant about adult information, but the rules are not the same when children are involved.

How they plan to use the information is usually not presented. Of the 38 sites reviewed by CME, a third had some kind of statement on how they were collecting and using the information. The remainder had no statement. Even the third with statements were not equal. Many contained limited information most often written for adults, not children. In one or two cases, adults might have had trouble understanding the statements. Parents' permission was rarely required, and when the statement suggested or encouraged parental permission, there was no way to verify whether or not it had been obtained.

A reasonable disclosure was on the Jazzy Girls site (www.jazzygirls.com). Its registration form explained: "It's easy to join the club, but you first must have your parent/guardian's permission. You have our guarantee that your personal information will go only to the people here at Binney and Smith, maker of Jazzy products, and to the agency producing this site. The information will only be used to allow us to create content that is geared towards the girls in the club. Your name and other personal information won't be shared with anyone else."[50] Notice the easy-to-understand language. This is written at a level appropriate for a preteen to understand. The statement makes clear that no third-party sales will occur and requests parental permission. The only shortcoming is that the site has no way to verify whether permission is asked and given.

Nabisco (www.nabiscokids.com), once in CME's *Web of Deception* report for poor notification, now offers a very extensive policy statement regarding the collection and use of information. While it does not obtain documented parental consent, it talks directly to minors in clear language. Nabisco recognized the unique capabilities of the Internet and has spelled out an ethical and fair policy.

Batman Wants You to Buy This

The gathering of personal information on Web sites capitalizes on children's natural willingness to talk about themselves. This makes children the gateway into the family for many companies. But another factor is at work. This is the building of a relationship with the child to induce loyalty and increase sales. One way to do this is to exploit product spokescharacters to create a relationship.

While children bond first with their parents, caregivers, and family members, before long they are relating to comic characters like the Power Rangers or Batman. These characters are important to children in their fantasy life. Although imaginary to adults, they are real and powerful trust figures to children.

Take these characters out of print and TV and place them on the Web where they can interact with your children, and you have a potent and powerful marketing technique. Companies and Web developers are aware of the effectiveness in a blended advertising/marketing/entertainment environment and aggressively utilize this methodology. The Mail Room in the Batman Web site invited children to send messages to Gotham City. Children could send the Batman characters e-mail messages and receive messages in return. This site (www.batmanforever.com) in 1996 conducted a survey where Commissioner Gordon, Batman, and all the law-abiding citizens of Gotham City asked your child to provide them with personal information. Children find it difficult to say no to these authority characters.

McDonald's Ronald McDonald (www.mcdonalds.com) wants your children to write him letters. Visitors to the site are asked to fill in the blanks to record first name, grade, favorite McDonald's food item, favorite sport, favorite sports team, and favorite book. Those who love Ronald won't want to disappoint him. The same is true of the M&M's characters: red, green, yellow, and blue. At one point in 1997, the M&M studio site (www.m-ms.com) featured a fictional world in which the visitor searched for the gray "imposter" M&Ms. As part of the "Imposter Hunt," the screen displayed a message from the "Security Department" asking for the visitor's help. In addition, the site offered an electronic "Imposter Hunt" poster if visitors would provide the name and e-mail address of a friend. Of course, children will respond to M&M's Security Department. And through their responses they become not only the gateway into their own families but into other families as well.

E-mail Messages from the Tooth Fairy

Many of these product spokescharacters not only communicate with children when the children are visiting the Web site; they e-mail them. One-fourth of the sites examined sent an e-mail message to the children after their first visit. To illustrate this, consider the Colgate (www.colgate.com/kids-world) site. Children visit the No-Cavities Clubhouse. From the clubhouse they could play a game, create a coloring book, get a mini-poster for a Brush Brush Brush! Chart, or talk to the Tooth Fairy™.

For many children, the tooth fairy is in the same league as the Easter Bunny and Santa Claus, mythological childhood creations. The image of a mythical being taking away baby teeth and leaving a reward is not one to be casually toyed with. Here the tooth fairy is used as an information collector turning children into good consumers. To be exact, the child is asked for name, age, and e-mail address. The submit button for this form reads "Put Your Tooth Under Your Pillow." In her summer 1997 FTC talk, CME's Pasnik told of following the directions on Colgate's No-Cavities Clubhouse site and receiving an e-mail message the next day. It said:

> Hi! I got your Email. I'm the Tooth Fairy . . . and I watch over your baby teeth.
>
> So, you've lost a baby tooth. That means you're growing up! It also means that now it's up to you to watch over your grown-up teeth.
>
> You need to take care of those new teeth coming in. They are yours for the rest of your life! Here are some of the tips I've learned; hopefully they'll help you too! Don't forget to brush your teeth at least twice a day with fluoride toothpaste. And visit my friend the dentist every year . . . that's really important! And my last advice is to limit your snacks. Healthy snacking is good but don't snack all the time!
>
> Now, it's up to you. Good luck! If you follow my advice, you'll help to keep your teeth healthy and your smile shining bright!
>
> Keep smiling!
> Your friend the Tooth Fairy.[51]

Good advice. But coming from the Colgate Web site, the line between advice and marketing is blurred, especially for the children getting the message. This blurred line helps companies cultivate the one-to-one relationship they seek without parental knowledge or permission. It goes beyond the visit to the Web site to include e-mail, a relationship builder. But the under-aged, no matter how much spending power they have, should be protected from being no more than consumers.

New companies are moving onto the Internet every day. To measure in snapshot form whether the problems were persisting, the Federal Trade Commission staff surveyed 126 Web sites listed by "Yahooligans!" a popular director of child-oriented sites.

While this was not a comprehensive study, the snapshot found:

- Eighty-six percent of the sites were collecting personally identifiable information from children (names, e-mail, postal addresses, and telephone numbers).
- Less than 30 percent had a privacy policy posted.
- Only 4 percent required parental authorization for collection information.

Recent findings like these call for further action. In March 1998 the FTC began conducting a systematic review of Web sites with plans to report to Congress on the extent to which they are employing deceptive and unfair practices in children's Web sites.

Children are grappling with the trials of growing up. This makes them vulnerable. Your children don't even understand that when they provide personal information to a Web site they are giving something away. (They probably don't even understand what personal information is!) Sophisticated advertising practitioners on the Internet are using their expertise and the tools of the Internet—cookies, harvesting, surveying, games, prizes, and sweepstakes—to obtain personal information and entry into your home. Further, they cleverly use product spokescharacters to gather information and to build relationships with your children. When coupled with e-mail, this can be a particularly effective ploy.

SELLING ALCOHOL AND TOBACCO TO YOUR CHILDREN

Before leaving this topic, one further warning is necessary. Alcohol beverage companies and, to a lesser degree, tobacco companies are a growing presence on the Web. Many are using the techniques previously described to appeal to a youthful audience. CME's 1997 report, *Alcohol and Tobacco on the Web: New Threats to Youth,* alerts us to the problem.

Under debate for years was whether or not R. J. Reynolds and other tobacco companies had specific strategies to attract underage smokers. No matter, the rise in youth smoking is undeniable. And underage drinking is a factor in all leading causes of death for young people aged 15 to 24. Advertising and marketing are playing a significant role in influencing the drinking and smoking behavior of youth.

In the report, 14 liquor companies and 10 large breweries with corporate Web sites use the techniques and methodologies we have reviewed. These include humor, hip language, interactive games, contests, chat rooms and forums, and product spokescharacters. Let's review some of the points in this specific area.

In the field studies, 16 out of 24 alcohol sites had some type of interactive game designed to keep visitors returning. The Cuervo Tequila Web site offers a slot-machine game called Beasts in the Blender, the Roadhog Adventure, and virtual Beach Volleyball. The Budweiser site features a game called "Trivia on Tap" in its "Thirst for Knowledge" section where visitors can test their retention of beer trivia.[52]

Product spokescharacters were highlighted. There was Captain Morgan on the Morgan Rum Web site, Budbrew J. (Bud) Budfrog, and Cuervo's J. C. Roadhog. There was also the friendly interactive bartender, Hank, living at the Amstel Web site. Hank is ready to provide advice to any visitor about life and its problems.

Chat rooms are very popular on these sites. This isn't surprising because chatting is one of the things people using the Internet enjoy, more and more. Advertisers like it because they can insert promotional messages subtly into discussions. A majority of sites in this report had bulletin boards, message boards, or chat rooms. The chat rooms created virtual environments emulating bars or clubs. The virtual environments had a party-down atmosphere with good times and drinking being the combination.

Tobacco Web sites were less uniform in the 50 sites examined. Very few sites overtly advertise cigarettes. Rather, Web sites are devoted to public relations. R. J. Reynolds' site has press releases about its corporate good works. Other companies, such as Eagle Tobacco and Seita Corporation, included financial information about the companies' sales and revenues with the press releases.

A number of "lifestyle sites" portray a glamorous smoking lifestyle. Instead of selling a pack of cigarettes, these sites sell the concept via a beautiful movie star smoking in a memorable movie. Lifestyle sites can be run by individuals as personal Web sites and can be commercially run. Both arrange for the visitor to have information on the smoking culture. Lists of where smoking is permitted, specialty brands, and often downloadable photos of celebrities smoking are there. Articles about smoking-related issues are also common. The message delivered in these sites is essentially this: Smoking is cool.

The best of the lot was the Smoker's Home Page, which included several sections that might appeal to young people. Examples included:

- Guide to Looking Cool When You Smoke
- Shotgunning and Smoke Bubbles Instructions
- Smoking-Related Audio
- Movies with "good scenes of ladies smoking"[53]

Two points should be mentioned about alcohol and tobacco Web sites, the first of which is not privacy related. A number of the commercial vendors sell alcohol products on the Web. Many of them are wholesalers distributing by 800 numbers or order forms. The customer's age is rarely requested. When it is, the customer simply clicks the button claiming to be 21.

The second point is a privacy issue. You certainly do not want your child giving personal information or interacting with spokescharacters from these sites. And you may feel safe. After all, you may think, your children wouldn't think of visiting Cuervo or Budweiser. Even if they did, you might well question whether they can spell the names correctly to get there. Can these sites, however, reach out and attract your child's interest and attention? Good spelling may not be necessary.

Search engine and directory companies are selling the rights to keywords and to positions on the "best sites" list. This provides companies an opportunity to be even more visible. By simply doing a search on key words like "contest" or "games," alcohol and tobacco links will pop up. This is easy access to a computer-literate child browsing the Web. Even more likely is a keyword search looking for free stuff like "screen savers." Half the sites offered free giveaways, usually downloadable screen savers. They would show up when this word is entered. So, even if your children have no proclivity toward alcohol and tobacco, they could innocently stumble onto one of these sites and be entranced with the talking frog or party atmosphere.

Pornography and molesters on the Web are a danger. In a very different way, so are the many sites designed to extract information from children and to sell to them. In both cases, the concern starts at privacy but moves further. Besides talking with and monitoring your children's Internet use, what other steps can you take?

The technology, which created this problem, also provides technologies for parents to use that could reduce it. In addition, new programs and possible legislation will make the Internet safer and more welcoming for your children.

7

HOW TO PROTECT YOUR CHILDREN'S PRIVACY

How can you create a haven on the Internet where your children can learn and play without fear of pedophiles and crass marketing practices? Continuing our special focus on children, this chapter looks at three avenues that have promise for a child-safe Internet: technology to block access to dangerous and undesirable Web sites, child-friendly and parent-approved policies and programs developed by companies on the Web, and new government activities and partnerships. Each avenue is presented and evaluated on its ability to protect your children from pornographers, pedophiles/molesters, and unprincipled marketers. The key will be to consider them with real parents and real children in mind. Technologists, corporation representatives, and government policy makers may devise elegant frameworks and sophisticated software. If the development is not family-friendly, it does not respond to your problems. While not one of these areas is an answer by itself, together they may create a tangible solution.

CHILDREN'S LEARNING AND DISCERNING ON THE WEB

On December 1–3 of 1997, the three avenues were debated at a White House Family Summit held in Washington, D.C. This summit brought together government and industry to explore the problems and concerns of parents and to seek solutions for a family-safe Internet. Speakers such as Vice President Gore, Justice Secretary Reno, and AOL Chief Executive Case expressed a joint commitment to creating an Internet haven.

Successful dazzling choices await families exploring the Internet, a convenient resource for any parent guiding family research efforts. Whether it involves finding a Web site in Cambridge, England, chock full of information for your seventh grader's report on the first computer scientist, Charles Babbage, or entails figuring out the best vacation for a family with a three-year-old and an infant, the Internet is an invaluable information and entertainment source for you and your family. Abundant information awaits you at the click of the mouse. And while learning can be fun, the Internet offers sheer pleasure in reading about the latest movies, comic book characters, and music stars—or playing the latest games, like Doom or War Craft 2. Unfortunately, the Internet can also shift to a sinister place that is not safe for your children.

The government, the private sector, and technology experts can all work together against pornography and perdition. Web sites' inappropriate collection of information from children for marketing purposes is a different issue. While future technology can certainly help, this issue demands that companies self-regulate, a most challenging proposition. The federal government has a role, too. It can encourage and coax; it can also threaten companies with regulation—an excellent attention-getter and motivator. And it may be necessary sometime in the future for the federal government to act. If the combined attempts of technology, industry self-regulation, and government beseeching fails, legislation may be required.

STAYING AWAY FROM PORNOGRAPHY

In a short time, more children than any other demographic group will be online. Children search for information, interact with their friends electronically, and form relationships with people without knowing the color of the others' skin or the accent in their speech. These activities are fun for children now and will prepare them to enter the workforce of tomorrow.

For children to flourish online, they must be protected from the harmful parts of the Internet, including sites with pornography. This is a daunting task; the number of pornography sites is enormous. While less comfortable with the computer and the Internet than their children, parents still behave as parents; they want to protect their children. A Jupiter research report based on researchers' conversations with children showed that:

- Sixty-two percent of the kids surveyed had some form of rules at home for when they were on the Internet.
- Forty-six percent reported their parents limit their time online.
- Forty-five percent said their parents restrict the sites they can visit.[54]

Parental control is the critical first step. You must engage in conversation with your children about the Internet and its hazards. The conversation should seek not only understanding of the hazards but should go further to set forth a framework of rules for using the Internet. This framework might encompass technology tools like blocking software to help parents monitor and reinforce the house rules. Recognizing that a framework or tools probably won't stop the most determined children from accessing inappropriate sites, technology can go far to establish control for most children. It is also not unreasonable to expect support and cooperation from the community and your government. This can be a boon for you and other parents wrestling alone with these concerns. And the industry itself has much to gain in market participation by developing a haven for families.

Parents—The First Line of Defense

Most parents take their jobs seriously. As you make rules and establish guidelines for your children's Internet activities, you look for information and ideas to ensure your approach will achieve the intended goals. The White House Family Summit announced several initiatives to support parents. One initiative the Department of Education is currently undertaking is to create a manual that will serve as a parent's guide to the Internet. The manual will point to sites on the Web that provide children with enriching, educational experiences and information. It will indicate sites you can turn to for help in setting up guidelines for your children's safe and productive Internet usage. The manual will be announced on the Department of Education's Web site (www.ed.gov) when available.

The Direct Marketing Association (DMA) has created a resource for parents already available on the Internet (www.cybersavvy.org). This Web site is designed to help bring you up to speed and teach you how to talk to your children about privacy and the online world. It begins with a set of questions to determine the knowledge level of the family then teaches you in an interactive way, using five different hands-on exercises you and your children can work on together. Then the site offers a tour of the Internet in easy-to-understand language. The "What Should I Do If" hands-on exercise is particularly useful for families since it creates real-life situations families may encounter on the Internet. For example: "While surfing the Web, I found a site with an interesting game that I want to play, but before I go any further, I have to fill out a form which asks questions about my interests and hobbies. What should I do?"[55] This gives your children and you a concrete situation to discuss. The discussion can reinforce your home rules on Internet use or help you in formulating rules.

Another initiative will be an outreach effort both for you and your children to increase awareness of the Internet's benefits and dangers. The outreach campaign will use as its identifier the rallying call: "Think Then Link." It will begin in spring/summer of 1998 with a series of public service announcements focusing on Internet safety that will target 71 million households. Another possible feature of this campaign is a televised "teach-in" showing families the hazards of the Internet and instructing them on safeguards. The program might even feature President Clinton or Vice President Gore. Combined, the public service announcements, DMA's Cybersavvy Resources, and the Department of Education manual will give you increased information and reinforcement to support your role as parent. Technology also can support the guidelines you establish for your children.

Technology Helpmates

The technology choices open today are in the early stages of their evolution. The one you may already be aware of is blocking software. Blocking software that is currently available operates on the premise of blocking speech, not access to sites. Parents enter in words or phrases and when the child attempts to type in those key words or phrases, the blocking software replaces them with Xs or erases the characters altogether. So if a child types in a web address "SEX," the software will not record the key strokes or will display "XXX." Although these software programs are first-generation technology, they are very good at blocking access to sites rated "Adult-Only." But they are not totally effective in avoiding all inappropriate sites for your children.

Many stand-alone blocking software products are on the market now. A sample of the products available are CyberPatrol, Cybersitter, CyberSnoop, GuardiaNet, The Internet Filter, Microsoft Plus for Kids, NetNanny, NetRated, NetSheperd, PlantWeb, Safe Surf, Specs for Kids, SurfWatch, Times Up!, and Triple Exposure. Each offers somewhat different choices or content categories to be filtered. The products range in price from free over the Net to $20 to $50 at retail software stores.

Several OSPs and ISPs offer free blocking software as part of their services. AOL, Compuserv, and Prodigy include a tailored version of CyberPatrol software. To check what your local provider offers, ask them directly or visit a Web site run by a nonprofit organization, Netparents, at www.netparents.org/isps/. This site lets you search for the ISPs in your area and see what parental controls they furnish.

If you do not have the option of using the blocking software provided by your ISP, finding such software in stores and installing it is not a straightforward process. To make software available in the retail market is costly. Roughly half a million to a million dollars is necessary just to begin to distribute it. And once you have it either from your ISP, the store, or company Web site, installing it can be challenging.

Like putting together those complicated toys on Christmas Eve, you'll most likely be optimistic as you review the benefits of the product and begin reading the directions for installation. But, your optimism goes downhill quickly when you sit down at the computer and the instructions tell you to go to the DLL files. Many of us haven't a clue when it comes to technical aspects of the Internet.

Eric Wenger, from the New York State Attorney General's Office, had just such an experience with his brother, much younger than himself. Wenger convinced his parents they needed blocking software to protect the younger brother from pornographic and other inappropriate Web sites. Because his experience at the State Attorney's office brought him into contact with cases and complaints about Web pornography, he knew of some awful stuff up on the Web. Wenger's brother was initially unhappy because he was intrigued by the thought of awful stuff, but older brother prevailed and mother and father agreed.

Wenger downloaded one of the blocking software systems and installed it, configuring it with different user IDs and passwords for each family member that would allow each different levels of access. He gave his mother and father unlimited access but restricted the younger brother. A day later, Wenger got a panic call from his father, demanding that he come home instantly. The father had forgotten his password and couldn't use the Internet. The family insisted Wenger disassemble the system—no easy task.[56]

Not everyone has this kind of experience. Many people are comfortable using blocking software. This cadre of people will expand as future generations of blocking software become easier to install and friendlier to use.

The next question concerns whether using blocking software actually does the job. Does it effectively block speech? Jeffrey Fox, assistant editor of Consumers Union (publishers of *Consumer Reports* and *Zillions*) investigated three popular systems—CyberPatrol, NetNanny, and CyberSitter. The investigative tests were designed by adults, but children actually played with the software systems to see if they could get around them. In one software system, the word to be blocked was the child's name. For the sake of the test, the name "Lois Lane" was used. The testers went to a site and the site asked for their name. The testers typed "lois" and the words were X'ed out. This would have been a good reminder to your children that they were not to give out their name. The tester children, looking to get around the software, typed "loi" and then before the "s" they inserted an "x" ("loixs"). The testers went to the next screen and then backtracked to the original screen with "loixs" on it. They deleted the "x." The software did not recognize the presence of "lois" because it was not originally typed as "lois." So, the children testers tricked the blocking software. This is termed an undisguised plot phrase. An undisguised plot phrase is not even an attempt at something clever. It is merely a typing trick.[57].

Only a quarter of homes with children on the Internet use blocking software now. As new generations of blocking software become available, they will be friendlier and more effective, and more parents will use them. In development now are systems that are built into your browser. You would have straightforward choices in selecting which sites would be off limits on your browser: Navigator or Explorer, for example. Control at the Web site level instead of the word level increases effectiveness because of the growing number of sites with new and unusual names. It can also avoid some of the tricks users can play when typing in words.

We are accustomed to having our movies rated, and most parents actively check the movie ratings before giving their children permission to see a film. Parents are ready to let their children attend a G-rated movie but want more information if it carries a PG rating. Most children don't even ask if the rating is R. The rating system is a tool parents can use to make decisions on what is appropriate viewing material. Recently television programs have introduced ratings that provide even more information. The television ratings indicate levels of both violence and sexually explicit programming.

Rating systems on the Internet are being developed, but in a different manner than TV or movies. The Internet, because of its size and diversity, can support multiple systems. Probably 30–40 percent of sites change or disappear periodically and new sites are being added constantly. Several rating systems are being developed and many are likely to be operating very soon. Some will be self-labeling. The Web operator will go to an independent third-party site and fill out a questionnaire about the content on the Web operator's site. The questions will ascertain the levels of sex, nudity, violence, and harsh language. Based on the answers, the third party will designate a label. RSAC is an independent third-party system that has labeled 35,000 sites. Safe Surf has labeled over 50,000 Web sites.

Other independent third parties will conduct their own investigations and assessments. Based on this, they will rate or label the site. NetShepherd employs a rating system approach similar to this and has labeled over 300,000 sites. Out of those, roughly 5–8 percent of the sites have adult-rated content. Independent rating or self-certified approaches can be valid if standards of labeling agree. The Platform for Internet Content Selection (PICS) is the technical standard developed by the World Wide Web Consortium. Multiple labeling systems, whether self-labeling or third-party conducted, that operate on the standards developed by PICS give parents the consistency they need. And it may be the way to deal with the problems of ratings on the Web. But it will take time and it will only be pertinent to U.S. Web sites.

Law Enforcement Gets New Partners

Technology can help avoid some pornographic sites on the Web. However, technology cannot prevent child molesters and pedophiles from interacting with your children in chat rooms or reaching out to them in other electronic modes. Law enforcement has a role in this arena and one that is very different from their traditions and history. The FBI when it was created 90 years ago did not authorize its agents to carry firearms. This quickly changed in the 1920s and 1930s when all agents were issued handguns and Thompson submachine guns. Today, FBI agents are issued laptop computers.

This is more than a symbolic gesture. The tools for fighting crime and the location of that crime has extended from the streets to cyberspace. Learning new approaches and techniques is the challenge federal law enforcement agencies as well as state and local police units face. They can be guided by those who know the terrain. One expert group in the workings of cyberspace includes the ISPs. Many ISPs have been unwilling to block access to discussions groups and World Wide Web sites that featured child pornography because of the desire to grant free speech. This attitude or approach has rapidly changed with an increasing sensitivity to the needs of families and a desire to have families fully participating on the Internet. Several large ISPs have promised to assist law-enforcement personnel who are investigating crimes against children, particularly pedophilia and child pornography. This spirit of cooperation may lead to a more potent policing of the Internet.

People actively using the Internet are additional resources to aid law enforcement. A new service, ready for operation shortly, has been created by the National Center for Missing and Exploited Children (www.missingkids.com). This new service is a "cyber tip line" for complaints about pornographic material, predatory behavior, and other illegal crimes involving children. According to the president of the Arlington-based center, Ernie Allen, if someone saw something illegal going on in cyberspace, he or she had no clear place to go.[58] The tip service, funded by the federal government, has a phone number, (800) 843-5678, and e-mail capability for people to report problems. The National Center for Missing and Exploited Children will relay the information to the appropriate authorities. This expands the reach of law enforcement.

FAIR PLAY IN MARKETING TO CHILDREN

The Internet does not have the same safeguards people are accustomed to with television, where the difference between program content and advertising is clearly delineated. They are clearly separate activities. The settings, sound level, and action are different. The characters in the content part of the program do not step into the commercial and begin selling.

This is not the case on the Internet, where no line differentiates advertising from content. Further, the Internet has the potential to be a more powerful marketing force with children because of its ability to engage users in interaction. The government and private companies are thinking through these issues and beginning the process of sorting out how to work together to avoid unnecessary regulation and provide families with a comfortable place. This process is being prodded by the Center for Media Education.

The Government Draws the Line on Web Marketing to Children

The Center for Media Education (CME) corresponds regularly with the Federal Trade Commission (FTC), a unit of the federal government specializing in protecting consumers against deceptive and unfair practices. The FTC Bureau of Consumer Protection had been given copies of CME's report, *The Web of Deception,* which detailed concerns about companies' Internet practices involving information-gathering from children. After this report, CME continued to provide the FTC with updated information on Internet information-collection practices that involve children. In May 1996, CME filed a petition requesting the investigation of and enforcement against one Internet Web operation, KidsCom. According to CME, KidsCom had violated the Federal Trade Commission Act Section 5, which prohibits unfair and deceptive acts and practices.

At the time of the filing, KidsCom's Web site (www.kidscom.com) required all visitors to register. The site was aimed at children ages 4–15 and described itself as "Communications Playground for Children." Registration involved the children answering question about themselves—their name, sex, birthday, e-mail address, home address, number of family members, and grade. After answering these questions, children had access to all the activities on the site. They could go to the chat room or be paired with other children for "pen pal" electronic letters. They could also check out the "New Stuff for Kids" section. This section discussed new products visitors might be interested in.

CME concerns fell into two categories. First, KidsCom did not provide disclosure information. Children visiting the site, and particularly children's parents, had no way of knowing what kind of information KidsCom was gathering, why it was collecting it, or how it planned to use the information. The other issue focused on the "New Stuff for Kids" section of the Web site. This was presented as an independent and objective look at various new products. KidsCom was endorsing these products based on its objective examination. However, these were not endorsements. The product manufacturers contracted with KidsCom to present the products on the site. Instead of endorsements, they were advertisements.

The FTC carefully considered this case. It is the first significant attempt on the part of the federal government to establish criteria on Internet information-gathering practices. In their investigation, they separated different forms of information collection and made distinctions. One distinct category is "personally identifiable information." In the FTC's view, using personally identifiable information required parental consent. Data collection for internal (Web site operation) purposes only and aggregated demographic data not linked to an individual did not require parents' permission. But, parents do need to be informed of the Web site's practices in these two areas. Beyond notice to parents, a method of control or opting-out should also be available.

In the KidsCom case, the FTC Bureau of Consumer Protection agreed that certain KidsCom practices did violate Section 5, but they did not recommend enforcement. They could not find any evidence that KidsCom had released personally identifiable information. But more compelling, KidsCom had modified its site in response to the CME's charges.

KidsCom now sends e-mail to parents. The e-mail provides parents with notice of collection practices. These collection practices are based on aggregated, anonymous data—not on information about specific children. Parents have the option to object to the release of information to third parties and can opt out. If parents do not use e-mail or the family computer, it is not clear how they will be notified.

The "New Stuff for Kids" section has been changed as well. The deceptive endorsement section has been removed. The section now clearly states that it contains product manufacturers' descriptions of products. KidsCom has even introduced a cartoon icon, the Ad bug, to identify advertising.

In a letter to CME's president, Kathryn Montgomery, the FTC promises to continue to monitor the situation and may in the future recommend law enforcement proceedings against marketers engaged in deceptive practices. Both the CME and FTC gained in this case. The signal was sent to Internet operators using unfair information-collection methods with their children visitors. The FTC articulated their analysis of principles—for aggregated data, notice and control; and for personally identifiable information, parental permission. And KidsCom responded. But hundreds of Web sites are directed at children. Investigating each and every one is impossible. This is especially true because new companies are moving to the Internet every day. Besides analysis and threats by the government, what else can be done?

Companies Move to Cooperate

Ideally, federal encouragement and threats could motivate companies to self-regulate. In this case, not only KidsCom was listening and responding. The Better Business Bureau (BBB) also responded. In 1995, the Better Business Bureau's Children's Advertising Review Unit (CARU) asked their board of advisors to look at the online environment and identify where new guidelines were needed. The advisors were leading experts in child development, education, communications, and industry leaders. The advisors took longer than expected and the critical issue identified was not the one anticipated; it was privacy. The advisors had expected issues like violence, sexually explicit sites, and other topics to occupy the number one position.

CARU designed and released the 1997 Self-Regulation Guidelines for Children's Advertising. These guidelines can be found on the Internet (www.bbb.org/advertising/caruguid.html). They include all forms of advertising but have pulled out interactive electronic media for special attention. These guidelines recognize that children may not understand the value or nature of personal information. It suggests advertisers adhere to the following guidelines in data collection:

- Before asking children for information about themselves or others, advertisers should remind children to ask a parent for permission.
- The advertiser should disclose, in language easily understood by a child, why the information is being requested and whether the information is intended to be shared, sold, or distributed to others outside of the advertiser company.
- If information is collected from children through passive means (such as navigational tracking tools, browser files, and so on), this should be disclosed to the child and parent along with what information is being collected.
- Advertisers to children who collect identifiable information online should make *reasonable efforts* in ensuring parental permission is obtained.
- Even if a child is asked to register at a site using his or her full name, advertisers should encourage the child to use a screen name like "bookworm" or "skater" in any activities that will involve public posting.
- If the information is optional and the child is not required to engage in an activity, that fact should be clearly disclosed in language easily understood by a child (for example, "Tell us your name if you want to").
- Since e-mail addresses can be used to learn other, personally identifiable information about the owner, e-mail addresses should be solicited on secure sites, when available. If a secure site is not yet available, an advertiser who solicits an e-mail address from a child should make *reasonable efforts* to ensure that parental permission is obtained.
- The interactivity of the medium offers the opportunity to communicate with children through electronic mail. While this is part of the appeal of the medium, it creates the potential for a child to receive unmanageable amounts of unsolicited e-mail. If an advertiser communicates with a child by e-mail, there should be an opportunity with each mailing for the child or parent to choose, by return e-mail, to discontinue receiving mailings.[59]

These guidelines cover many of the concerns expressed by the CME and the FTC. According to Elizabeth Lascoutx, vice president/director of the CARU, in her testimony before the FTC during the summer 1997 privacy hearings, all the major players have complied with the guidelines. If the Better Business Bureau is successful in having its members adhere to these guidelines, great progress will be made in creating a haven for families. But, remember, these guidelines, as thoughtful and comprehensive as they are, are just guidelines or goals. The Better Business Bureau does not have an enforcement mechanism.

Some companies will adapt the guidelines and appreciate the guidance. But the worry of many is that bad actors (companies that do not respond to guidelines or FTC analysis) will remain. This is trouble for everyone. It is trouble because Web sites are linked to one another by hyperlinks. These hyperlinks let a child move from one Web site in compliance with the Better Business Bureau Guidelines to another that is ignoring the guidelines. The move is seamless and the child may not even realize he or she has moved to a new site.

These concerns are valid. Is it too early to make decisions? If it works, self-regulation will be much faster and flexible than government regulation or enforcement. Perhaps the concluding thoughts in the FTC ruling on KidsCom were correct: Monitoring the situation is the important next step.

THE EDUCATOR'S NEW CLASSROOM ASSISTANT

President Clinton and Vice President Gore have campaigned to link every school and library to the Internet by the turn of the century. Students of the future will be proficient at using word processing programs, navigating a World Wide Web site, using an Internet search engine, and compiling a spreadsheet—all before they enter high school. By adding Internet capability to schools, educators will have a rich source of information to help them and their students.

For creative ideas in curriculum planning, educators can turn to the Internet. There are several sites offering teachers ideas. For example, the University Corporation for Atmospheric Research with funding from the National Science Foundation has a Web page designed for middle school mathematics teachers with 16 classroom activities to take place over six weeks using real-time weather data. Another site, www.covis.nwu.edu, has curriculum plans in the science area including *Mining Your Own Business* (geology and mining) and *Shake, Rattle, and Roll* (earthquakes).

Not only do these sites suggest curriculum, they provide a group of classroom tools to make the topics more realistic and often more interesting. Students can access satellite data and pictures to study the earth and its environment. Live remote sensing data from cargo ships at sea can be obtained for studies of routes and navigation. When the Internet is incorporated into curriculum with knowledgeable teachers, the learning taking place in the classroom is enriched. The Internet can help students in study situations too. E-mail volunteer programs and telementoring projects guide both children struggling and those seeking more.

When children are using the public school or library Internet connections, the concerns about privacy are no longer a family issue. They become a community and education system concern. Educators must think through the privacy worries of parent, students, and teachers. But they must extend their thinking to assess the privacy risks as seen by the school board, taxpayers, and the community at large. To warm up to the issues in a general way, review the Federal Trade Commission's introduction to privacy, "Site Seeing on the Internet" at www.ftc.gov/bcp/online/sitesee/index.html. This overview is only a foundation. Incorporate it into the foundation choices in technology and good practices for a school or library policy before problems arise.

In the children's arena, there are tools and support for you in dealing with pornographic Web sites or companies with deceptive marketing practices. Technology, company self-regulation, and government threats of action all intermingle and support each other. Can these three tools be of use to adults in their search for Internet privacy overall? The next three chapters return to the adult world and take each technique and explore its potential and short falls. Technology will be discussed first. You already know about technologies that invade your privacy. It is now time to learn about technologies to protect and enhance your privacy.

8

TECHNOLOGY—THE CAUSE AND CURE OF THE PRIVACY PROBLEM

Returning to the adult world, technology is used by government and businesses to obtain personal information about you. Invasive technologies track your personal behavior in quiet and invisible ways. When you visit Web sites, Web operators record what you look at and for how long. They may even deposit a cookie into your hard drive to help them record information—perhaps over repeated visits.

At the same time, technology can also be a tool to protect and enhance your privacy. It can shield you from the prying eyes of Webpeepers when you send e-mail or visit sites on the Internet. This chapter discusses two such technologies, anonymizers and encryption, reviewing what these technologies do, when to employ them, and what their limitations are. The difficult political issue of encryption will be highlighted as well.

In addition to acting as a shield, technologies can facilitate your decisions about when providing personal information is appropriate and when it is not—based on the collection, use, and disclosure policies of the Web site. This gives you realtime control over the flow of personal information when you browse the Internet. The World Wide Web Consortium's Platform for Privacy Preferences (P3P) is currently developing a realtime control system.

ANONYMIZERS

When your identity is revealed, or can be readily figured out, digital technology can collect vast amounts of data about your communications and interactions.[60] One way to minimize or eliminate the collection of your personal data is to keep your transactions anonymous. Consider a costume party invitation. The host knows who was invited even if he or she cannot tell which guest is which. But imagine if, instead of coming dressed as a gorilla or the Phantom of the Opera, you were able to be invisible. The host now has a different problem. He or she does not know if the invisible person is there at all. You can listen to conversations, read private notes, and even eat the best snacks, and no one is aware of your presence. Anonymizers make a person invisible. Another way of thinking about this is that anonymizers protect you when you surf the Web or send e-mail by acting as the middleman or proxy.

Why would you want to be anonymous? Perhaps you plan to place a personal ad and want to be very cautious. Or, you may have opinions you want to express on bulletin boards or in newsgroups and are concerned that others will be intolerant of your views. Or maybe you want to search for sensitive information related to a medication you are taking for depression and want to make sure your employer doesn't find out. These and other related reasons call for the use of an anonymizer.

The services can vary. Take the last instance—you don't want anyone to know that you are searching for and retrieving documents on a certain subject. You have the Web address. In this case, you could contact the anonymizer run by Infonex Internet Services, a leading provider of Internet privacy services. Last year over 7,000 people routinely used this service and the number of users is growing. You can contact this service at www.anonymizer.com and ask them to obtain the document for you and e-mail it to whatever address you provide. No one will know it was you who requested the document. This service offers a free trial for those interested in exploring the possibility of anonymity on the Internet, and carries a modest fee for regular service.

Perhaps you want to arrange for anonymous e-mail because you do not want the parties you interact and communicate with to know who you are. Anonymous Remailers will take your e-mail and remove all identifying information. The remailer will then forward the message. Such systems give you an anonymous address where people can send you mail. The remailer will then forward these messages to you. The people sending you messages will have no way of knowing your true name, location, or ISP. A good source for information about remailers is www.well.com/user/abacard/privacy.html. This is the home page of Andre Bacard, author of *Computer Privacy Handbook.* On his privacy page is a list of practical privacy FAQs (Frequently Asked Questions) and facts including information about anonymous remailers. This site explains in simple terms the ways to use a remailer and the differences between remailers. In fact, the first question answered in the fact sheet is: "What is a remailer?"

The most famous remailer is anon.penet.fi. Over 50,000 people use this system for a variety of purposes. Anon provides a unique identification number to its users, but the security in the system is not rigorous. Other more secure possibilities include www.replay.com/remailer/ and www.nymserver.com/. But beware; some users of these systems are engaged in pornography and other illegal activities. One more thing: The anonymous services you use will know what you are looking at and who you communicate with, so make sure they are trustworthy.

At times anonymous behavior is not called for, but keeping the information itself secret and confidential is. This calls for encryption.

ENCRYPTION

Cryptography is the ciphering and deciphering of messages in code. To cipher or scramble a message is to encrypt it. Remember using "pig Latin" in front of your little brother and parents when you were a child? In pig Latin, the first letter of a word was moved to the end of the word and then “a” and “y” were added. So hello became “ellohay.” While you may have amused yourself and confused your siblings, your parents probably recalled pig Latin from when they were kids! This elementary cipher has its roots in a long tradition of codes.

Scrambling messages so enemies and eavesdroppers could not understand them has been done throughout history. The first recorded examples appear in ancient Egyptian hieroglyphics. The idea of scrambling a given set of data according to a mathematical key was introduced in Roman times. Caesar reputedly used the simple substitution cipher (for example: “a” is replaced with “c,” “b” is replaced with “d”) to send messages back to Rome from Gaul.[61] Many of the world’s earliest computers were developed to break codes. During World War II the German’s advanced encrypting hardware, the Enigma, was broken only when researchers at England’s Government Code and Cypher School developed an even more sophisticated machine to cipher-break the Enigma codes.

Today junior high school students with home computers could easily break the codes that won and lost wars in history. And the tradition of cryptology, particularly encryption, has moved from specialized purposes such as spying and warfare to common usage on the Internet. Internet users will, at times, want to guarantee that only the person for whom their message was intended reads the document. Or, the Internet user may want to be confident that the document was not tampered with in any way and arrived to the intended person without slight or sly changes being incorporated.

Beyond personal uses of encrypted files, you may want others in companies or government to encrypt your data at times. For example, organizations managing your medical records may use encryption to ensure privacy. So, too, might organizations that deal with your financial information. And when those organizations provide your information over the Internet, encryption makes sure cybersnoops do not have access to documents that are none of their concern.

The encryption technology used today had its beginnings in the Engineering Department of Stanford University where Whitfield Diffie and Martin Hellman first developed a feasible way to encrypt and exchange secure data over insecure channels in 1976. Three young professors at

MIT built on the Diffie-Hellman work. Ronald Rivest, Adi Shamir, and Len Adleman collectively invented a cryptographic system that is the basis for the public-key system used today.

Public-Key Technology

The public-key technology has a mathematical basis with which we are all familiar. Somewhere between fifth grade and seventh grade, we are introduced to the math concept of prime numbers. A prime number can only be divided by itself and the number 1. So 7 is a prime number whereas 4 is not a prime number since it can be divided by 2. There is an infinite number of prime numbers.

Now it gets trickier. Multiply two prime numbers. For example, if you multiple the number 7 and 11, your answer is 77. Both 7 and 11 can be divided evenly into 77. This is termed "factoring" the number. It is not terribly difficult to factor 77. But what if the two prime numbers multiplied together were large and the product of the multiplication was huge? Then you would need a computer to figure out the original two prime numbers. Bill Gates in his book, *The Road Ahead,* gives the example of 11,927 multiplied by 20,903 with the product number being 249,310,081.This difficulty in factoring enormous numbers underlies an ingenious kind of cipher.[62]

Keeping these basic principles in mind, the public-key coding system uses two different decoding keys—one public key to encipher the message (the product of two prime numbers multiplied) and a private key to decipher (the prime numbers themselves). Both keys are related. Since the enciphering key is based on the product of two huge prime numbers, even though it is public and known, its size makes it impossible to factor it into its two prime numbers even with computer help.

Now the practical applications of these two keys are at the heart of computer encryption technology. Each user's computer will use prime numbers to generate an enciphering key. This will be a public key because it will be listed publicly. In Gates' book, he provides this illustration: "I have information I want to send you. My computer system looks up your public key and uses it to encrypt the information before sending it. No one can read the message, even though your key is public knowledge, because your public key does not contain the information needed for decryption. You receive the message and your computer decrypts it with a private key only it has. It corresponds to your public key."[63]

This concept became known as the RSA cryptosystem. RSA stands for the first letter in the last names of those three MIT professors: Rivest, Shamir, and Adleman. They used products of prime numbers so large, they projected it would take millions of years to factor a 130-digit number. They were so convinced it was impossible that they issued a worldwide challenge to anyone interested and daring. This project became known as the RSA Inc.'s Cryptochallenge or RSA 129. A 129-digit number was used to encrypt a message. The message was available on the Internet and soon computer scientists and cryptographers from around the world were working in a coordinated fashion. A total of 600 people from 24 countries with the help of 1,600 workstations combined efforts to meet the challenge, but it took eight months before the code was broken. The two prime numbers used to form the 129-digit product were found. One was 64 digits long and the other was 65 digits. And the message itself was: "The magic words are squeamish and ossifrage." (Ossifrage is a large predatory bird.)

This united code-breaking effort was impressive. Nevertheless, it took almost a year to decipher the message. And, RSA Inc. only had to add a few more digits to the product to make it much more difficult to crack. Now, a 250-digit product is believed to take over a million years to factor, no matter how many people or what amount of computing power they could use. One last point: Because the number of prime numbers is infinite, running out of public keys or duplicating them will never be a problem.[64]

Individuals and companies can use encryption to protect privacy and safeguard personal information. Encryption can have another important use—to prove you are the person you say you are. Currently, you cannot enter into contracts on the Internet because you would have no way to sign and notarize documents. But encryption can be used to create a digital signature.

This is not a "digitized" signature. Rather, like an encrypted document, it is a series of numbers and letters that appear to be random. As with public-key technology, a public and private key is used to translate the signature. When deciphered, the signature must match exactly to be valid. This secure system, once recognized legally, will permit legal and contractual activities to occur over the Internet with assurance that the parties engaged in the activities are who they claim to be. These elegant encryption systems can be extended to the common user and everyday e-mail. The extension is a software program that is almost a political statement.

Zimmerman's PGP

Phil Zimmerman loved secret codes. As a boy, he learned Morse code and Braille and practiced making invisible inks and code wheels. As he grew older and left for college, he replaced these interests with physics, computers, and politics. He did return to his enjoyment of codes and picked up again the study of encryption. In 1977, he read Diffie and Hellman's work with excitement. That same year he read the article in *Scientific American* by Rivest, Shamir, and Adleman about their encryption concept.

By the mid-1980s, Zimmerman became concerned that unless large numbers of people began using cryptographic programs to protect their privacy on the Internet, cryptography would remain in the control of the government. The government might even move to curtail people's access to strong cryptography.[65] The system developed by Rivest, Shamir, and Adleman (RSA) was not right for widespread use by large numbers of people in applications like e-mail. It required too much computing power. The computational power needed for RSA was only available then in places like MIT or Stanford University.

Working 12 hours a day for over six months, Zimmerman appropriated and combined these powerful academic discoveries. He amalgamated the Diffie-Hellman system, RSA, and a standard secret-key encryption system to produce a program that is easy to use and essentially uncrackable. He worked with zeal because he was concerned the government might outlaw private cryptography before he could finish his program. At that time, 1991, the Senate was considering a bill banning public use of cryptography.

The program, Pretty Good Privacy (PGP), was fast with sophisticated key management and digital signatures. As a plus, it was user-friendly. Zimmerman decided to make the program available for free. Computer scientists around the world loved the program. And it was delivered before Congress could legislate prohibitions against encryption. Now encryption was not the sole domain of the government. It was cryptography for the masses!

Elation was brief for Phil Zimmerman. He was faced with major problems on two fronts. The president of RSA Data Securities, Inc., Jim Bidzo, threatened to sue Zimmerman on the grounds of patent infringement if he didn't stop distributing PGP. Although Zimmerman complied, it was too late. The program was so great that it had received attention from cryptographers around the world and was multiplying ferociously.

The second front was from the government. U.S. law gives private citizens the right to use encryption products. Even though the law permits an individual's encryption products, the National Security Agency (NSA) was not happy. Their top scientists could not crack PGP. NSA and other government agencies were uncomfortable with people having codes they could not decipher. They were even more concerned that enemies of the United States might obtain those codes. It was against U.S. law for encryption products to be exported. It was the export issue that launched a federal investigation in 1993 and a federal grand jury probe against Zimmerman. By 1995, the government finally relented. Although PGP had been exported, it had been exported by a colleague who posted it to a Usenet newsgroup for cryptographers, not Zimmerman.

The issue is still under debate with the government law enforcement agencies and national security organizations concerned about encryption capabilities for private citizens. The FBI has been vocal about its worry regarding organized crime. Encryption lets criminals operate on the Internet and law enforcement cannot stop them. When criminals use the phone lines, law enforcement can use wire taps. There is no equivalent to wiretapping with encryption unless the FBI knows the codes.

Law enforcement and intelligence concerns are being considered by Congress in a very unusual manner. The FBI and its colleagues in government enforcement and intelligence have agreed to encryption such as PGP and the other programs on the market. But they want to have the keys to those systems. And in future systems, they want a back door where they can enter. Congress will debate this issue this year and in the future. And it will be the first time Congress has argued about limiting the privacy of all its citizens.

MAKING PRIVACY DECISIONS EASY

You will have times when you will want to seek information or communicate anonymously. You might have documents or messages that require the use of encryption tools to ensure the information is seen by only the intended reader and is not tampered with or changed in any way. But, these situations will occur infrequently. Most people are usually faced with a more mundane problem, that of deciding your privacy preferences and executing the decision regularly.

Thinking about how you want your personal information to be handled cannot be avoided. It is a personal decision because people vary in their privacy needs. Ask yourself the following questions:

- Are you comfortable with a Web site gathering personal information if it is only used for internal purposes like product development or Web site enhancement?
- Can a Web site sell your personal information to a third party if it has aggregated it so it cannot be traced to you?
- If a company is going to sell your personal information and it is personal—your name, address, and interests—is it going to let you know to whom and why? Is the company going to compensate you?

How you answer these questions will give you a framework for a privacy preference system with which you are comfortable. While this is a difficult exercise, the execution of your privacy preference system is even more challenging.

When you visit a Web site, you hope the site has a privacy statement or policy. A good privacy statement/policy tells you what kind of information the site is collecting, why it is collecting it, and how the collected information will be used. Ideally, the policy will continue and provide you with some choices. Choice possibilities include letting you review the information gathered or not participate at all by opting out. Today, you would have to check every site you wanted to visit to see whether it had a privacy policy. You would then have to read the policy to make sure it conforms with your desires. This is a time-consuming process and an opportunity for technology to help.

A technology tool that helps you decide in a seamless and automatic way whether a Web site complies with your privacy preferences is exactly what is needed. Two groups, working together, offer the future solution—an automatic preference system built into your computer browser. Next, we will explore the work under development by the Internet Privacy Working Group and the World Wide Web Consortium's Platform for Privacy Preferences leading up to this system.

Speaking the Same Language

The Internet Privacy Working Group (IPWG) is a broad-based U.S. coalition of information providers, advertisers, software developers, and consumer and online advocates. This coalition is defining a privacy vocabulary. A common set of terms lets Web operators and visitors expect the same thing. For example, when a Web site requests contact information, what does that mean? It may be asking for name and address. Or it may be looking for cyberspace contact information, an e-mail address. Determining agreed upon definitions ends this confusion and provides reliable expectations. The ability for both parties to express themselves and be understood is at the heart of this activity.

In this system, you can express what you want; you can convey your choices about how to handle your personal information. Web site operators are not forced to comply with what you want, but they now have a language to communicate whether their policies for information-handling match the visitor's wants. Technology can use the common language to develop a tool to make this matching process occur quickly and effectively.

Facilitating Privacy Preferences

For the past two years, the IPWG has worked closely with the World Wide Web Consortium, W3C. W3C is an international organization founded in 1994 and hosted by MIT's Laboratory of Computer Science, the Institut National de Recherche en Informatique et en Automatique in Europe, and the Keio University in Japan. Over 180 members from around the world form this consortium. The activities of W3C include promoting standards, serving as a repository for information, and developing various prototypes and sample applications to demonstrate new technology. The Platform for Privacy Preferences project, P3P, is a prototype of a new technology.

P3P working together with IPWG is aimed at facilitating the matching process. The goal is to develop a thoughtful but easy-to-use system built into the computer's browser to serve as a decision-making tool. Web site visitors do not have to read each and every privacy statement to find out whether its policies adhere to their desires; P3P will do it for them. The system is still in the design and demonstration phase. The specifics of this description will most likely be refined and fine-tuned, but the following review will give you a feel for what the designers are attempting.

Using P3P, you would go to your browser and select the Privacy Preference File Choices. An example of this is shown in figure 8.1. The choices that appear on the screen will range from having access to all Web sites to wanting to visit only sites that do not collect any information. In-between selections could be sites that collect information for internal use only, or sites that collect information shared with third parties. You would make your selection from the various options. Every time you went to browse the Web, the privacy preference file would inform you whether the site you want to visit adheres to your choice.

Here is an example the W3C director, Tim Berners-Lee, uses to explain how this system would work (see figure 8.2). A user, in this case a high school student, had selected the choice that lets sites collect information only if they use the information internally. The student is now looking at Web sites to get information about possible colleges. One college site the student visits does not comply with the choice. A screen or

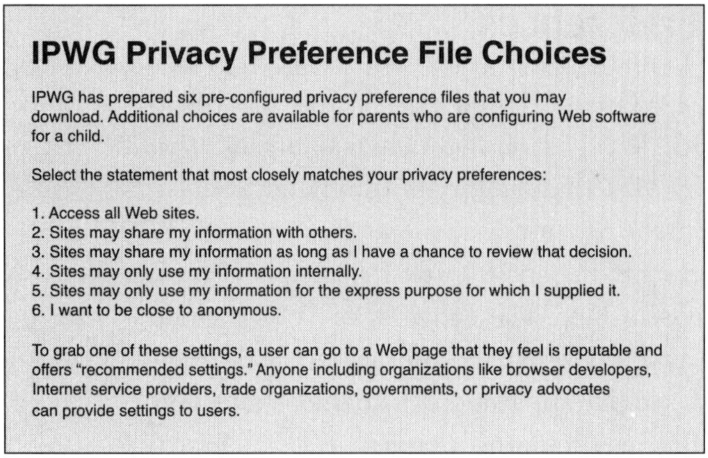

FIG. 8.1:
Privacy Preference File Choices

Source: www.w3.org, Copyright World Wide Web Consortium (Massachusetts Institute of Technology, Institut National de Recherche en Informatique et en Automatique, Keio University). All Rights Reserved

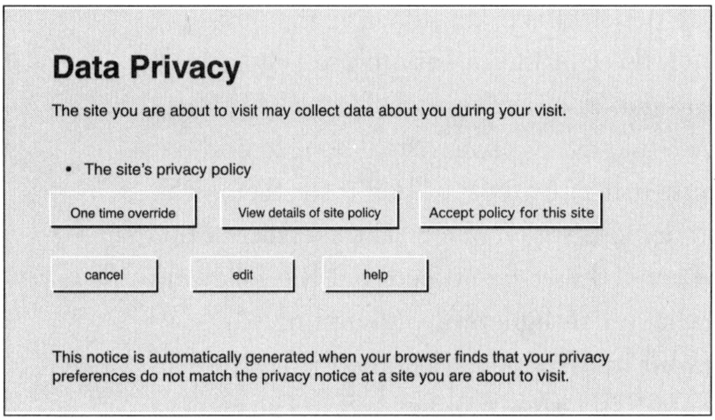

FIG. 8.2:
Data Privacy Choices

Source: www.w3.org, Copyright World Wide Web Consortium (Massachusetts Institute of Technology, Institut National de Recherche en Informatique et en Automatique, Keio University). All Rights Reserved

dialogue box would appear to inform the student that information is going to be requested and used in a way the student has not accepted nor given his or her consent to. The screen would give the student a number of options. One option would be to look at the privacy statement of the site. If the student clicks on this, reads the policy statement, and decides to accept the policy, he or she would then click a button to accept the policy and then view the Web site.

The student may decide immediately on another choice and simply move to another site. On the other hand, he or she may decide it's worth the risk to go directly to the site even if it does not meet the original

Privacy Preference Files for Children

Although there is no substitute for going online with your child, this is not always possible. In order to ensure that your child fully benefits from the wealth of resources available on the Internet, you may wish to make some choices about how your child's personal information will be handled online. Because no two children are alike, you will want to consider your child's age, level of maturity, and understanding of interactive technologies as you set in his or her privacy preferences.

Select the statement below that most closely matches the Internet privacy preferences you have for your child:

1. I want my child's online privacy to receive the maximum amount of privacy protection.
2. My child can visit Web pages that collect information as long as it cannot be tied to his or her real identity.
3. My child can visit Web pages that collect personally identifiable information for internal purposes only.
4. My child can visit Web sites that share personally identifiable information with others.

It's important to remember that when your child discloses his or her e-mail address or other personal information in public forums such as bulletin boards or chat sessions, a Web site cannot control how other visitors use it.

Your browser software may allow you to supply a password that will be required to change or override the settings you make for your child.

FIG. 8.3:

Children's Privacy Preference File Choices

Source: www.w3.org, Copyright World Wide Web Consortium (Massachusetts Institute of Technology, Institut National de Recherche en Informatique et en Automatique, Keio University). All Rights Reserved

choices. The P3P is actually facilitating the negotiation between the student and the Web site.

The platform can have features to enhance children's privacy as shown in figure 8.3. On the browser, you and your children can review and select file choices. The choice menu would be similar to the figure above. The operation of the system would also be similar. If your child wanted to go to a prohibited site, he or she could talk to you to get permission. So instead of having a system where the child cannot type in the site he or she wants to visit, you now have a system that simply will not permit a site that doesn't match your children's privacy preference to show up on the screen. This control at the browser level is more flexible and robust.

P3P will save time in screening or matching your choices with the Web site's practices and will not limit users. You can override or skip the choice you made to look at a site that does not meet the original criteria. It does what a decision tool is designed to do: facilitates part of the process to be efficient and negotiates part of the process to be effective. The P3P will be ready for full-scale demonstration soon. Its success will, of course, depend in part on its ability to match and negotiate. Participation of the community of Web site operators, advertisers, and developers is essential.

Companies operating on the Internet need to provide the fundamentals of notice and choice. This can be done via a privacy statement for those operating Web sites and through other vehicles for the professional reference service providers. Notice and choice are not enough. Oversight and enforcement will be required to engender consumer trust. Are companies ready to provide the information you need to make decisions about privacy?

9

CORPORATE CYBERSNOOPS FACE THE MUSIC

Because the Internet is new, the rules of doing business are not yet defined. Companies are looking for input to shape their practices. In the privacy arena, they are getting information from you and the U.S. government. How these two forces are shaping the actions of companies is detailed in this chapter. The chapter first examines the professional reference services or look-ups and evaluates their self-regulation efforts. While this investigative effort focuses on 11 companies, we will also take a broader look at companies in general on the Internet, their Web sites, and their voluntary privacy protection activities to see if they develop privacy policies that will keep you coming back.

Companies realize the Internet is part of their future. It offers wonderful opportunities to expand its customer base and profits while reducing the costs of doing business. As a customer, you can always come to the Net, regardless of where you are or what time it is. You can move around the company's Web site without help from a company representative. If your experience is a positive one, you will mark the site and come back again and again. And each time you return, you build a relationship with the company. But the success of Web relationships, as in many other relationships, will depend on trust.

FRIENDLY PERSUASION

The individual reference services (IRS—not to be confused with the Internal Revenue Service) are vital to commerce in this country. Considering the large and growing number of people living in the United States, employers, credit firms, and others businesses must verify that the person with whom they are interacting is indeed who they think they are interacting with. When J. Roberts applies for an X-ray technician position you are offering, you would hope it is the certified technician J. Roberts—not the Hollywood actress, Julia Roberts. A reference service will confirm this for your company—quickly—so you can make the hiring decision.

While such services clearly benefit companies, some disturbing aspects of reference services trouble individuals. The concerns people articulate include:

- Is the information about you accurate?
- How can you find out what is written about you?
- How can you correct the information if it is wrong?
- How can you prevent the information from being misused?

These are legitimate concerns for which there were no satisfactory answers until recently. Then in 1996, the seeds for a self-regulation initiative in this industry were planted; and in December 1997, the individual reference services industry announced it had developed voluntary privacy protection guidelines that would respond to individuals' mistrust and fears.

On October 9, 1996, Christine A. Varney, then Commissioner of the Federal Trade Commission (FTC), spoke to a large group of businesspeople at the Privacy and American Business National Conference. She explained that the FTC was created to protect consumers from unfair and deceptive business practices. Continuing, she stated that privacy for consumers was a critical part of the FTC's protection responsibilities. To make sure the audience understood her message, she said:

> Today, personal information about an individual is being collected at a rate and to a degree unthinkable even five years ago. Currently, much of an individual's personal information can be legally collected, shared, exchanged, sold, and disseminated without notice or input by the individual. . . . In short, the time has come for us to consider whether the existing arrangement properly balances individual personal privacy values with competing information flow benefits.[66]

The audience listened to the public message and agreed that a new privacy balance that emphasized notice and choice for individuals was necessary. The compelling attention-grabber in this message spoken by a commissioner of the Federal Trade Commission, which had the power to pursue regulation and to prosecute offenders, could not be ignored. No company wants to be saddled with cumbersome rules and requirements. Perhaps some in the audience thought or hoped this was a one-time public issuance or that Varney was simply floating an idea for discussion. Just how serious was Varney?

Very serious. Varney followed her public statement at the conference with a continuing string of motivating actions. She spoke privately to the corporate officers of IRS companies. In her conversation, she encouraged them to organize themselves and respond in a positive manner to the public's concern about the way the reference services operated. She warned that if they did not step up and regulate themselves, the federal government would.

It is unclear which—the encouragement or the warning—proved the successful inducement, but the result was IRS industry action. In March 1997, Lexis-Nexis, with the help of outside counsel, Ronald Plesser, contacted all the major players in the IRS industry and brought the key ones together for a series of meetings designed to develop voluntary guidelines. Over 10 months, the 14 companies listed in figure 9.1 worked to devise a plan that would appease the FTC, consumers, and their boards of directors.

Acxiom Corporation	CDB Infotek
DCS Information Systems	Database Technologies
Equifax	Experian
First Data Solutions	IRSC Inc.
Information America	Lexis-Nexis
Metromail	National Fraud Center
OPEN	Trans Union

FIG. 9.1: Participants in the Individual Reference Service Voluntary Privacy Program

The companies involved in this effort represented about 90 percent of the industry. Three were the major credit bureaus—Equifax, Experian, and TransUnion—companies that supply all the information to the reference service industry. Experian and TransUnion are active suppliers or wholesalers of data; Equifax is less so. All are already regulated by the Fair Credit Report Act.

In the middle area are First Data Solutions, Inc. and Metromail Corporation. While not credit bureaus nor regulated, they have supplies of information available for distribution. First Data Solutions, for example, is a global company processing credit card information for VISA, Mastercard, and others.

The remaining nine companies are information distributors or vendors. Some, like Lexis-Nexis, are global, while others have a national audience such as Information America Incorporated and CDB Infotek. A few are regional companies like Online Professional Electronic Network (OPEN), which mainly operates in the Midwest. The distributors are split, based on their client base. Some distribute information to businesses only and others have directories for the general public. All 14 companies are active users of private electronic networks and the Internet.

Privacy Principle No. 1

The agreement the 14 companies drew up responded to many of the issues voiced by the FTC, privacy advocates, and consumers. Three privacy principles were the center of the agreement. The first was the standard of accuracy. Incorrect information is dangerous in this environment—especially when aggregated with other information, shared, and replicated. In the process, the errors do real harm. Further, it is unlikely the individual affected will even know the source of his or her problems resulting from the errors!

A hospital interviewing for a staff physician or chief of surgery is going to reject applicants whose professional license records are mistakenly excluded from a professional licenses database. An entrepreneur seeking a line of credit from the bank will be turned down if his or her records have been crossed with those of a convicted white collar criminal with the same name. [67] Consumers, unaware of IRS companies in general and especially not alert to the dangers of data file inaccuracies, are sometimes puzzled why their credit was not extended or why they did not get the job offer.

The voluntary guidelines respond to this issue. Since the sources of the information are the three credit bureaus, the first step is to ensure that when the credit bureaus transmit the information to the vendors/distributors, the data transfer is 100 percent accurate. It may be that the file the credit bureau transmits has a mistake, but the mistake must not change when the information is transmitted. This ensures that the vendor has the same information as the originator, the credit bureau. The consumer can go to the vendor and request his or her file. Because this industry is not widely known by consumers, public education and an outreach campaign are needed to educate consumers on what information the IRS companies have, how the information is used, and how to find out about the information contained on each individual. The outreach campaign will be accompanied by general advertisements and postings on the companies' Web sites.

Once the individual has contacted the vendor and requested his or her file, the individual may see errors and want to correct those mistakes. The guidelines permit this only with nonpublic information. The IRS companies are not responsible for errors from public information sources. If the data file an individual receives has an error in reporting from the individual's driver's license or a *New York Times* article, the individual would work with the public sources (in these cases the Division of Motor Vehicles or the editor of the *New York Times*) to correct the information.

When the vendor is notified of a nonpublic data error, the service will correct the error or inform the individual of the source of the incorrect information so the individual can pursue correction if out of the IRS' scope. The IRS vendor will then correct the error by making sure the correction becomes part of the credit bureau's database. Since the credit bureaus are the suppliers of information, the correct information must get back to them. With the corrected information entered into their systems, replication of mistakes or continuing inaccuracies is prevented.

Privacy Principle No. 2

The second principle responds to unlawful uses of the information contained in these databases. Unscrupulous customers or employees, scam artists, or corrupt Internet surfers could unleash substantial damage if they could obtain personally identifying facts and files. The Secret Service reports one such case. Labrar Folarmi claimed to be the owner of a home-improvement business. He obtained an account and an electronic link with one of the credit bureaus, Experian. The Secret Service suspects he downloaded over 500 credit reports. Using those reports, he and his associates engaged in "identity theft." The victims had their bank accounts drained and their credit card accounts run up. Before Folarmi was stopped, he allegedly stole more than $250,000.[68] Experian spotted his frequent use of the database, terminated his service, and reported the activity to authorities. This was a bold and direct crime with serious financial repercussions.

The information available from IRS companies could inflict punishment in a physical manner. Stalkers and abusers have used IRS services to find the whereabouts of their victims; the predator who tracked down and murdered actress Rebecca Shaeffer at her front door used a private investigator to access her records and find her address.

Resolving the problem of unlawful use of information required careful thought. The IRS proposed a resolution in its guidelines by creating three tiers of service. These three tiers are summarized in figure 9.2. The first tier of service is available to the general public. Any citizen is able to get

Qualified Subscriber
Detailed Nonpublic Information
Careful Screening

Professional and Commercial User
Limited Nonpublic Information
Screening

General Public
Name, Address, and Listed Phone Number
No Screening
Opt-Out

FIG. 9.2:
Three Tiers of Service

this information, but the information itself is limited; it does not include Social Security numbers, date of birth, unlisted phone numbers, or mother's maiden name. It will include name, address, and phone number (if listed). Individuals can opt-out of this database if they wish.

The second tier of service is for professional and commercial users. Although Social Security numbers will not be displayed (or will be truncated if they are), more non-public information will be available than in the general public service and there is no opt-out option. For example, the month and year of birth will be accessible. The professional or commercial user has to prove to the IRS that they are an established business entity and agree to the terms and conditions of information use. They are required in advance to state the purpose of the data they seek. Purposes will depend on the company. Lawyers will use this tier of service to find witnesses, marketers to verify the accuracy of their customer lists, and banks to detect fraud.[69]

The third tier of service is devoted to carefully selected "qualified subscribers." The IRS companies will conduct a review of the candidate subscriber and the intended uses of the information to determine appropriateness. Law enforcement agencies and private investigators using the information to locate suspects or search for missing children illustrate appropriate users. The candidate will sign an agreement limiting the use and dissemination of the information. Qualified subscribers, although carefully screened and tied to enforceable contracts, will be rewarded with access to detailed nonpublic information. As in the professional and commercial users' service, individuals cannot opt-out.

The tiered system balances the amount and type of information with user constraints. For a broad pool of users, the information is minimal. The audience narrows based on the qualifications necessary to obtain access. If companies meet the qualifications, they can obtain more information. If they can meet the highest standards, they can obtain the most detailed information. As the level of information increases, the restrictions increase as well.

Privacy Principle No. 3

All the laudable principles combined are meaningless if there is no way to ensure that they are enforced. Privacy advocates have this concern about any self-regulation effort. The 14 companies involved in this effort have agreed to an enforcement plan. All company members must undergo an annual compliance review. The compliance review cannot be performed by the companies themselves. An unbiased third party must conduct the review.

Independent review provides the oversight and enforcement element lacking in many self-regulation configurations. It is a plausible plan, but will it work? No one knows. The Federal Trade Commission and the members of the program plan to revisit the issues in 18 months. Both the FTC and self-regulation participants can then assess the guidelines' operational success in balancing consumers' privacy with the benefits of information flow. It's a worthwhile test. But it is a test.

WEB OF TRUST

The IRS industry has a significant role to play in making people more confident of their privacy in the Electronic Age. So, too, do the millions of Internet sites in operation and new ones that appear daily. These sites collect information with your active participation; they learn about you when you fill out surveys, register at Web sites, and enter contests. Companies also learn about you in secret ways. They collect information without your knowledge, using a number of different tracking technologies, including invisible tools such as cookies.

You do not like it. The U.S. marketplace in general has the lowest consumer satisfaction ratings ever.[70] Although a number of factors contribute to this phenomenon, one is the loss of control consumers feel over their personal information. Companies know they do not have an optimum selling situation when their market target, the consumer, is discontent and feeling vulnerable.

The Direct Marketing Association (DMA) recognizes this. The largest trade association for businesses interested in direct marketing and database marketing, the DMA has over 3,600 corporate members in the United States as well as members in 49 foreign countries. A large number of DMA's member companies are embarking on efforts to build Internet businesses. They see the benefits. Amazon.com, an Internet bookstore, increased its sales by nearly 10 times this year, selling 6.5 million books. Internet airline ticket sales nearly tripled and are expected to grow sixfold to $5 billion a year by the year 2000.[71] Other companies want to join in the enormous growth of electronic commerce. To do this, they will need consumers' trust and confidence. This means facing consumers' concerns about privacy.

Robert Wientzen, president of the DMA, separates consumer privacy issues into those based on fear and those that result from anxiety. Some privacy issues fall into the category of fear: understanding a danger and having a legitimate concern about it. Wientzen, however, believes the more compelling issue is anxiety—fear of the unknown. If companies eliminate some of the unknowns, consumers will increase their trust.[72]

DMA's activities have been concentrated on working with their member companies to communicate to consumers about notice and choice. Last year DMA, in conjunction with the Internet Services Association, developed draft guidelines covering notice and choice. In January 1997, DMA formally accepted the privacy guidelines, which state that Web sites should:

- Disclose what kind of information they collect
- Explain how the information is being used
- Provide a legitimate mechanism for consumers to use to prevent their information from being shared with third parties

Each member received a copy of the guidelines. An aggressive campaign with the rallying cry—Privacy Action Now—began to reach out to members and help them understand the importance of the guidelines and the need for action. Coupled with the Privacy Action Now campaign, an online tool helps companies communicate their privacy policies to consumers. The tool, located at www.the-dma.org, is easy to use.

Privacy Online Help for Web Operators

This resource is a template of a privacy policy, which is filled in based on the visitor's answers to a series of questions. A Webmaster or Web site operator can respond to the nine questions in a matter of minutes. This is the key to the tool's effectiveness: The right questions are asked. For example, question number 3 covers the type of information collected, such as domain name, e-mail address, specific Web page(s) accessed or visited, and data from a site registration or survey. Question number 4 lists the following six ways in which the gathered information could be used:

- Use for internal review
- Web page content improvement
- Customizing the content and/or layout of Web pages for individual consumers
- Notifying consumers about Web site updates
- Sharing with other organizations to help them contact consumers for product development purposes
- Contacting consumers for marketing purposes

After the visitor has filled out the answers to the questions, the online tool will convert the answers into a privacy policy. The policy can be e-mailed to the visitors, Webmasters, or Web site operators so they can circulate it within their company for improvement and approval. Or it can be delivered in a fully compliant HTML-formatted page, ready to be put up on a company's Web site. A steady stream of visitors have used this tool. Examples of users include small startup companies, government groups, newspapers, international direct marketing trade associations, educational institutions, nonprofits and associations, Fortune 500 corporations, and even a few gambling businesses.

Companies have no excuse for not having a privacy policy. This tool makes creating a privacy policy a straightforward proposition. And the privacy policy should be truthful. If the company does not accurately reflect its practices in the collection and distribution of personal information, it is in violation of the Federal Trade Commission's deceptive practices rule and can be charged.

When Encouragement Is Not Enough

The privacy guidelines have been given to members. DMA's outreach campaign and Internet online privacy policy tool has begun to galvanize members to implement the guidelines. DMA has decided to go beyond encouragement. By July 1, 1999, DMA will insist that all of its members comply with its privacy guidelines. Honoring the principles of consumer notice and opt-out will be mandatory from that date. So will the use of in-house suppression lists, which are listings of people who do not want to receive information from the company. The suppression list is acted on by the company and forwarded to DMA. If member companies do not comply, the member will go through a process that will result in its expulsion from DMA.

Wientzen expects 80 percent or more of its members to have and be enforcing privacy policies by summer 1998. The rest, he feels, will be motivated by the July 1 ruling and quickly respond. But not everyone is as optimistic as Wientzen. A 1997 study commissioned by DMA found fewer than one-third of the members surveyed had implemented the privacy mechanisms set out in the guidelines.[73] For membership compliance to go from 33 percent in 1997 to 80 percent in mid-1999 will require a major jump.

YOUR SCORECARD ON SELF-REGULATION

The initiatives in self-regulation are part of a new phenomenon with no success formula to follow. You will want to watch these initiatives to see whether they are meeting your privacy requirements. You'll want to evaluate them in two areas.

The first is awareness. You need to know who is collecting your information, what it is to be used for, and how you can limit its disclosure. DMA's plan for privacy policies placed on Web sites is responsive to your need to know. Check to see whether the plan is working by looking for changes on the Web sites you visit. Are they providing you with more information on privacy issues? The individual reference services also comply in their plan with your right and need for awareness.

Beyond notice, you deserve choice. The opportunity to exercise choice on how personal information is used should be readily available and user-friendly. This will be an area to watch in both self-regulation initiatives. For the IRS initiative, the requirement for straightforward mechanisms to request and correct personal information, as well as to opt-out are necessary. Both initiatives will pioneer systems, which may need refinement, modification, or complete overhaul!

The second area for you to score and evaluate is enforcement. You deserve assurances that Web sites will comply with the rules of the initiatives and that you and others have recourse if they do not. The Department of Commerce's National Telecommunications and Information Administration developed draft guidelines on the elements of effective self-regulation (www.ntia.doc.gov/privacydraft/198dftprin.htm). This discussion piece identifies these three elements of enforcement:

- *Consumer Recourse:* When a problem occurs with the self-regulation initiative that affects you, the companies involved should offer ways to resolve your complaint.
- *Verification:* Proof that companies are indeed doing what they promised is a vital part of self-regulation.

- *Consequences:* Companies that do not sustain their self-regulation commitments should face repercussions. Types of repercussions include cancellation of association membership, entry on to a "bad actors" list, and even government action. The repercussions do need to be evenhanded and immediate to reinforce to other companies participating in the initiative that meeting their commitment is important.

In the two initiatives presented, this area has been defined; but it is still early. Since neither initiative is fully in operation, you do not know how effective the initiatives' enforcement procedures will be. The IRS initiative has mechanisms for compliance: the third-party audits and a FTC review of progress. DMA threatens its noncomplying members with disqualification in 1999.

Both are starting points, but it is unclear whether either will be satisfactory. Keep your scorecard handy over the next 12 months. If these self-regulation initiatives do not meet your requirements, you may want to raise your voice.

REACHING OUT TO INVOLVE EVERYONE

And what about the sites operated by non-DMA members and the companies not involved in the IRS initiative? How can they be reached and urged to respond to privacy issues like notice and choice? One way might be through consumer pressure. When consumers view companies as enemies, companies do not profit. Enemies, unlike friends, do not respect privacy or confidentiality. Another possible avenue might be the marketplace itself. Companies are learning how to interact on the Internet. Many are bringing the practices and approaches they used in the physical world to cyberspace. Those practices include obtaining demographic information about customers even when it is not clear how this information will be used. In cyberspace it may be unnecessary to know the visitor's name, address, age, and income; perhaps the only pertinent information is the visitor's interests.

The private sector is not alone in developing Web sites that are responsive to your privacy desires. The Social Security Administration made highly sensitive personal information available on their Web site. The exceedingly rocky road leading to this Web service containing your intimate financial information is told in the form of a case study. The story is without doubt a cautionary tale.

10

YOUR PRIVATE FINANCIAL INFORMATION IN THE PUBLIC DOMAIN

Is responsible handling of personal information on the Internet possible today? This chapter examines the possibility using a case study of what happened to your personal and private financial information when it was moved from a government-controlled massive database to the Internet. This case covers very sensitive personal information maintained by the Social Security Administration and should resonate with most readers. It moves through two years of the development, launch, and results of an Internet application and notes the thoughtful practices as well as the mistakes that were made.

At the core of the case is the issue of control privacy concerns. The chapter demonstrates the care developers took to secure the information. Securing information with passwords and encryption is different from letting you control your personal information. When people are not given notice and choice about their personal information, they react.

YOUR EARNINGS AND THE INTERNET

The application discussed in this chapter involves the area we are most sensitive about—personal financial information. It is the Social Security Administration's (SSA's) move to make our earnings and estimated benefit information available over the Internet, an effort affecting all of America's 150 million workers and 48 million beneficiaries.

The government is experienced, even a leader, in providing information over the Internet. Over 1,000 Web sites are maintained for the executive branch of the government alone. This approach provides citizens with information that is public and cost effective. The SSA case study does not, however, focus on presenting public information; it presents *private* information—your earnings and estimated benefits. Before beginning the case study, some background on the SSA's history is necessary to set the stage.

SSA—The Early Days

President Franklin D. Roosevelt signed the Social Security Act in August of 1935, as seen in figure 10.1. The act was a response to a concern he and others had about the welfare of our citizens. The Depression years had been difficult, filled with economic failures and uncertainty. This insecure environment prompted the president and Congress to develop a framework to protect the average person from job loss and a poverty-ridden old age.

The president and Congress created a social insurance program that had several provisions for general welfare and a program to pay retired workers aged 65 and older. This was landmark legislation in one significant way: It was the first time the U.S. government required citizens to provide personal information. The public was not happy. Many felt this was an unwanted intrusion into private lives, a sentiment reflected in the newspapers of the day.

FIG. 10.1:
FDR signs the Social Security Act on August 14, 1935

Privacy Concern About the Program

A New York newspaper on November 2, 1936, showed a man stripped to the waist, wearing a dog-tag. The dog-tag represented the identification all workers would have to show so the government could keep track of them. The story reported that this was the fate of anyone participating in Social Security. The visual is depicted in figure 10.2.

But newspapers went further than reporting these concerns. They fed the public's worries with massive amounts of misinformation and rumor. Press reports claimed Social Security would gather information about a person's religion, union affiliation, criminal record, medical history, and other data.

The Boston American reported: "Your personal life will be laid bare. Your religion and the church you attend will be listed. Your physical defects will go down in black and white . . . Your union affiliation will be stated . . . Even your divorce, if you have one, will be included."[74] This story even included the "official government form" used to obtain this information. Since stories like this one showed up frequently, Social Security's first test was to build the trust and confidence of our citizens.

In November 1936, the day before Social Security numbers were to be distributed, the SSA released their first press announcement. The statement heralded the following policy: "Only the worker himself, or his

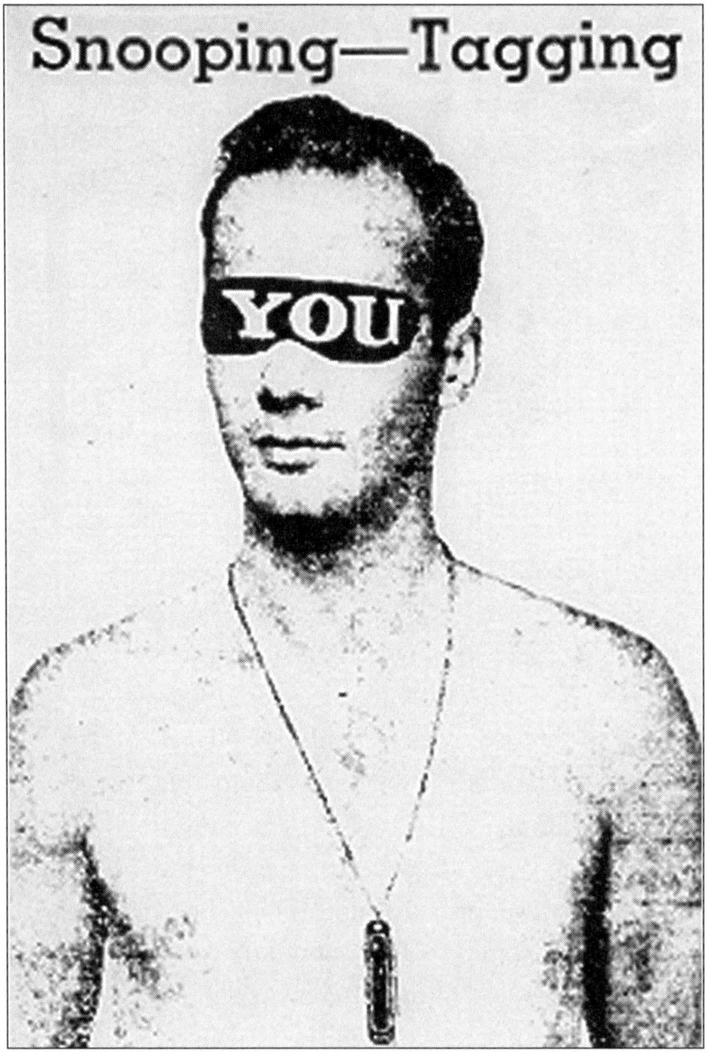

FIG. 10.2:

Snooping and Tagging

Source—The New York American

immediate family, or government employees having official responsibility in connection with the Social Security files, will have access to this information." This policy was clarified a month later with the two sentences: "The Board will, at all times, regard the information received from an employee as confidential. The files will be open only to those who have a legitimate interest in the administration of the Social Security Action."[75] The second statement was the straightforward declaration many citizens were waiting for.

These press announcements were followed in 1937 with Social Security's first regulation. Entitled "Disclosure of Official Records and Information," it reviewed the process for maintaining confidentiality of personal information. The regulation mandated that employees could not release information—no matter who requested or demanded it. They could not supply it even in the case of a subpoena. The employees were to follow certain procedures if such requests were to occur, including filing a report directly to their supervisors.

These press releases and the regulation helped relax the public's tension. Some complimentary news stories even started to show up. An example is the *Washington Star* article published on April 29, 1937, which said: "No wives need apply to the Social Security Board for information about their wandering husbands . . . nor can a lover find out his girlfriend's actual age from the card-index files . . . No power on earth can pry from the Social Security Board any information whatsoever . . . Not even a member of the Cabinet, and particularly Attorney General Homer S. Cummings, in whose department the G-men flourish, is permitted to see a single file at the Social Security Board. . . ."[76]

THE INTRODUCTION OF A NEW SERVICE

Time passed and the Social Security Administration expanded. In 1988, a new service began called the Personal Earnings and Benefit Estimate Statement (PEBES), which was conceived as a tool to help individuals and their families plan for retirement. The PEBES statement shows the salary history of an individual, upon which Social Security payments and other benefits are based.

What Is a PEBES?

A PEBES includes:

- A year-by-year listing of the Social Security–reported earnings

- A year-by-year listing of the Medicare contribution reported
- An estimate of retirement benefits at age 62, at full retirement (currently age 65), and at age 70
- An estimate of how much the worker would receive in disability insurance benefits if disabled now
- An estimate of survivor benefit amounts for spouse and children if the worker died

It does *not* contain three important elements:

- The requester's mailing address
- The name and address of the requester's employer
- Current-year earnings

This statement could indeed be valuable in helping plan a financial future. In order to obtain a copy, people would ask for a form by phone or mail. The form consisted of 10 questions to be answered. The questions were similar to those you would find in any situation intended to verify identity—that people were who they said they were. In fact, Social Security reviewed the policies and practices of the banking industry and used them as a model. The information requested was:

- Your name as it appears on your Social Security card
- Your Social Security number
- Your date of birth
- Other Social Security numbers you have used
- Your gender
- Other names you have used
- Estimated earnings last year and this year
- The age you plan to stop working
- The average amount of money you expect to earn between now and the time you stop working

After providing this information, the form asked you to fill out the address you'd like your PEBES sent to and to sign and date the form. You could expect your statement in about six to eight weeks.

Three to four million people a year requested their statement by mail. The feedback was positive; those using the tool appreciated it. The system of delivery seemed to be working adequately, too. Over the decade, no serious incidents of fraud were reported.

NEW LEGISLATION BRINGS NEW CHALLENGES

But then a significant change happened. Two pieces of legislation passed in 1989 and 1990 placed a tremendous challenge before SSA. Public Law 101–239 (passed on December 19, 1989) and Public Law 101–508 (passed on November 5, 1990) obligated the SSA to provide all workers who are 25 years old and older a copy of their PEBES every year starting in the year 2000. This could exceed 120 million statements.

The legislation permitted a phase-in or build-up time. By 1995, workers 60 years old and older started to regularly get their PEBES. By the end of fiscal year 1996, 12.5 million automatic PEBESes had been sent out with a target of 70 million by the end of fiscal year 1999. Congress felt that putting this information in the hands of taxpayers on a regular basis would be valuable, especially for younger workers in making decisions about finances and retirement early in their lives. Congress also hoped the administration could correct mistakes early, thus avoiding difficult situations.

A difficult situation is just what one woman encountered. She had a serious disease and could no longer work. But when she checked into the amount her disability would cover, it was painfully low. An investigation ensued and investigators found that she had been using the wrong Social Security number for the past 10 years. Her earnings and the resultant benefits were being credited to the actual holder of the Social Security number she was incorrectly using. They caught the error and corrected it. Ninety-nine percent of SSA earnings records are properly posted, but the wrong number or name will create a mistake. PEBES is a way to catch those mistakes, which can make a difference in the average retiree's benefit by $75 or more a month.

How the Internet Got into the Act

With the goal of providing this useful tool to help all Americans in their financial planning, SSA considered how to deliver the PEBES in a way that was accessible and cost effective. In addition to using the U.S. Postal Service to deliver, the Internet was suggested as a possibility. The SSA was encouraged during the initial examination of this delivery mechanism. The Internet offered citizens a convenient way to get their statement and would be inexpensive for the SSA.

Based on costs from the past few years, the SSA estimated it would cost about $5.23 to mail each report. Using the Internet, delivering the same report costs a fraction of a penny.[77]

In the initial plan, people could request their PEBES on the Internet and the SSA would mail it in the traditional manner to the address provided. This combination of traditional and new delivery systems was developed over two years. It was expected to lead into a full deployment of the online system where an individual would request and receive their statement online. The first part of the development process focused on security.

DEVELOPING A SECURE ONLINE SYSTEM IS NOT ENOUGH

SSA is a member of CommerceNet, which is funded by the federal government and is a consortium of government and private sector companies seeking to foster secure Internet commerce. Through this group, SSA had access to the leading computer companies, financial institutions, community access organizations, and academics all focused on security technologies and secure Internet services. In addition to using the resources CommerceNet and its members provided, SSA commissioned an extensive study of the vulnerabilities of an online PEBES by a security team at Los Alamos National Laboratory.

This study examined the risk posed by electronic vandals. It assessed the methods these vandals or hackers would use and suggested design, technology, and training measures to counteract the risks. Taking these suggestions and others from the various committees in which SSA participated, its own security response team designed a secure gateway (computer firewall) to protect the SSA mainframe from unauthorized access via the Internet. SSA hired professional consultants to test the gateway, using a variety of penetration tools and techniques. While the gateway held and could not be breached, this exercise suggested other security measures, including restricting access to key directories.[78]

Another safeguard built into the system was encryption. The e-mail messages were encrypted—electronically scrambled—between the sender and receiver so if a computer hacker intercepted them, the result would be gibberish. The encryption process used works with at least a 40-bit electronic key. When tested, it took 250 computers, with the capability to test 100 billion code combinations an hour, more than three hours to break the code.

The system was set up so the Social Security auditors could trace any request for information back to the computer that originated the request. This created an audit trail of sorts. By locating the computer attempting to get unauthorized information, SSA hoped to be able to catch the person operating the computer, the perpetrator.

With security measures in place, the SSA began initial tests with the public. The pilot program had individuals request a PEBES online to be mailed to the addresses they provided. San Francisco was the site of the pilot program from March 6, 1996, to April 16, 1996. SSA then opened the test to full Internet participation on April 17 through August 16. In the full test, SSA got 4,000 comments with a majority indicating they appreciated being able to use the Internet. Those being tested appreciated this convenient way of obtaining information and the fact that it took less time than the traditional method. By calling or requesting the form in writing, then sending it back, the lapse time for actually getting the PEBES was six to eight weeks. This system of ordering online reduced response time to between two and four weeks.

Privacy Issues at Public Sites

In the course of these tests, the CommerceNet members did bring up a privacy issue for people who obtained Internet access at public sites, such as libraries, where other users might be able to view or retrieve information inadvertently left on the machine.[79] To rectify this potential problem, new features were added, including a warning about criminal penalties for fraudulent use of the service. Those using the PEBES system see the following statement on the computer screen: "I understand that if I deliberately request information under false pretenses I may be guilty of a federal crime and could be fined and/or imprisoned." Depending on the statute, imprisonment could be up to 10 years. This care with protecting information follows the pattern of concentrating on *concrete* concerns and security, not on *control* concerns.

Testing the System

In the fall of 1996, the SSA tested the full online capability for meeting the needs of individuals requesting and obtaining their PEBES. Throughout all the development, SSA assumed the service would be used by the Web-aware. And in fact, it was the computer literate who participated in the tests. To verify the corrective measures, the tests took place in libraries in the twin cities of Cedar Falls and Waterloo, Iowa, and later in Baltimore County, Maryland. The people tested were volunteers on a regular visit to the libraries or who visited because of local media articles.

Feedback was enthusiastic. After entering the request into the online system, individuals were rewarded with the PEBES response. This immediate delivery resulted in positive comments like "This was too easy! Is it a trick or something?" Direct observations of the tests echoed the excitement with only a few comments expressed about security or privacy. One problem SSA anticipated did not happen. The Administration was concerned that when individuals did not get matching records, the individuals would assume SSA had lost their records instead of the possibility that they entered incorrect or incomplete information. This situation did not occur. Volunteers understood the matching concept.

Still in the testing phase, SSA went national with the complete online PEBES in March 1997. It did not advertise the service because it wasn't ready for vast numbers of people using the system. But it did need to in-

Information needed to obtain a report:
• Full Name
• Social Security Number
• Date of Birth
• Place of Birth
• Mother's Maiden Name

FIG. 10.3: Information Needed to Obtain Online PEBES

crease the volume of participants beyond those in the limited site tests. The increased volume would help establish usage trends and see how well the system worked.

A person using either the PEBES by mail (batch system) or the complete online system was asked to provide certain authenticating information (see figure 10.3): name, Social Security number, date of birth, place of birth, and mother's maiden name. This authentication process was consistent with the existing process in the 800-number call-in and written request procedures, except that both of these require a form with signature.

From March to April 1997, 71,000 requested the complete online PEBES. The age profile of the requesters followed the standard bell curve, with most being in the 45–55 age range. The young computer whiz kids the SSA expected were not highly represented. Of the 71,000 requests, SSA provided only 47,000 PEBESes online because the other 24,000 requests failed to pass the authenticating process. The primary reasons 30 percent failed to pass were mismatches of mother's maiden name and the requester's place of birth. Anecdotal evidence indicated that many failed attempts were harmless, caused by a requester striking a wrong key or by misspellings.[80] Mistakes in input were taken into account when designing the system. When recording the answers to the five pieces of information, seven errors could occur with the ability to correct them. But the system did not instruct the user which elements were wrong. This was done intentionally to make it difficult for anyone relying on guesswork.

Besides the denied access, the system detected multiple requests coming from the same computer. When these were investigated, there was usually a reasonable explanation. In several instances, it was a financial planner obtaining information on behalf of several of his clients. In other cases, the requests originated from a library or university computer. The inspector general of the Social Security Administration, David Williams, traced a single Internet request back to a university computer and learned that as many as 3,000 students had access to this computer.[81]

THE UNPLEASANT SURPRISE

After careful planning and development, SSA officials were pleased with the way PEBES Online was going. While balancing security and access, it was providing citizens with their personal information in a convenient and responsive manner. The system was also proving as cost effective as officials had hoped—a plus for the SSA and taxpayers alike.

In the development process, SSA incorporated all the features it knew users would want. What the SSA did not incorporate, because it did not anticipate the need, was notice and choice. SSA failed to recognize how important controlling personal private information is to Americans. Even if their information is kept secure, people want to be told what is happening and be given a choice to participate or opt-out.

What SSA did not know, they learned quickly and painfully. In early April a flurry of newspaper articles appeared, led by a front-page article in *USA Today* on April 7. The articles raised serious questions about privacy and suggested the new system had compromised the financial privacy of Americans.

Exploitation of Fears—Shut Down Access

Evan Hendricks, privacy maven and activist, warned in articles: "As soon as crooks start exploiting this service to get other people's information, Social Security is going to have a real problem on its hands." Who are these crooks? They could be legal adversaries, an employer wanting to know about an employee's outside income, or an ex-spouse looking for an adjustment in support payments.[82]

And according to the articles, it would not be difficult for them to pose as someone else and obtain the salary information they seek. The five areas used as authenticators are not hard to discover. A Social Security number can be uncovered by information vendors or a private detective. Court papers and records of marriage licenses and divorce decrees often contain mother's maiden name and date of birth. Some of this information may even be recorded in the state's vital statistics department.

And the penalty declaration on the screen is not a deterrent to the person who is after your personal information. The audit trail could lead investigators to the computer used, but not to the person behind the computer. With access to the Internet available at schools, libraries, and even cafés, tracing the person could be extremely difficult.

The articles hit a cord with many Americans. The availability without notice or choice of financial information is threatening. Financial information, particularly salary information, is highly personal, and people want to be in charge of it. When personal financial information is combined with the Internet, emotions intensified. One man immersed in a legal suit was worried his opponent could find out how much money he made and use this as a basis for suing him for even more money. Another was certain the wife from whom he just separated would find a way to get his PEBES and use it against him in court. And a woman did not want her co-workers to know how much she made in comparison to them.

The threats and emotions they created rose. So did misinformation and rumor. Stories began to circulate that hackers could break into the SSA through the PEBES Online system and gain access to other SSA records. Statements were made that PEBES could have avoided all this trouble if they had been smart enough to encrypt the information. None of this was true. Hackers could *not* gain access to other SSA records and the system *was* encrypted. One woman called an SSA official with her fear. She was living in Asia and did not want her relatives to be able to trace her. She was anxious because she thought the PEBES Online would help them find her. This is another example of the terrible worries people have when they feel they have lost power over their personal information.

In the two days after the *USA Today* story, the number of people logging on to PEBES Online skyrocketed—50,000 visited the site. Such an increase is a standard phenomenon. The result was akin to a newspaper story describing a neighborhood so safe no one locks their doors at night. Revisit the neighborhood after the story has been published, and you'll find that burglaries and theft have escalated dramatically.

Even discounting misinformation and rumor, the SSA recognized they were losing the trust and confidence of the public. Their critics were compelling in their arguments. SSA had not sufficiently anticipated or planned for individual privacy protection. There is certainly some overlap between security and privacy; and SSA did well in the overlap areas. But it had emphasized security, getting solid security advice from CommerceNet and Los Alamos National Laboratory. The Online PEBES was indeed secure, but privacy—your control of your information—was largely forgotten.

On April 9, 1997, before the public's perception got any worse, Acting Commissioner John J. Callahan suspended temporarily the online interactive PEBES test. Although SSA had not involved privacy experts and representatives in developing the system, they decided this was the time for a fresh review and open discussion.

RETHINKING THE ISSUES

To that end, SSA announced a series of public forums across the country over a 60-day period to obtain input from specialists in computer security and privacy. It hoped consumer advocates and the public would come forward and participate. SSA would listen carefully at these sessions and emerge with a clear vision of the next steps to take.

The forums took place from May 5 to June 16, 1997, in six cities: Hartford, Connecticut; Des Moines, Iowa; San Jose, California; Austin, Texas; Atlanta, Georgia; and Washington, D.C. The format for each meeting was identical. Three panels with three to five members each participated. Privacy experts and consumer advocates made up the first panel; the second panel consisted of computer technology experts, especially security spe-

Privacy Panels
Lack of easy-to-use method of authentication that ensures privacy
Balance expense and convenience of security measures with risk of disclosing personal information
Consumer Scams - particularly with older Americans as targets
Business Panels
Current safeguards (firewalls, encryption, and secure socket layer) are sufficient
No difference in fraud patterns on the Internet vs. other banking methods
Banks have been conducting secure transactions on private networks for over 20 years
Technology Panels
100% security does not exist
Consider some form of PIN and password as identification
Public-key technology may be future solution

FIG. 10.4:
Select Panelists' Issues

cialists; and the final panel was comprised of business users of the Internet, primarily in the banking and financial planning areas. The forums were open to the public and offered periods of time for public comment and questions.

To encourage public attendance and interaction, SSA publicized the forums in each city. It used public service announcements and paid notices in the local media. The SSA Web site, Social Security Online, carried detailed information about the meetings. The panelists, agenda, times, and location (and even a map to each location) were available on the Web site. Even with this outreach campaign, public participation was low.

The 60 expert panelists, however, provided thought-provoking discussions of issues, and SSA did receive 6,000 comments e-mailed in from citizens. Figure 10.4 groups and summarizes many of the issues brought forward at the forums.

In listening to the experts, SSA officials had to determine the key issues and evaluate them. Then SSA officials had to make the final and most difficult decision: Should PEBES Online continue? SSA had to choose between (1) modifying PEBES Online and continuing to offer a complete Internet system, or (2) disbanding it and relying on the batch system that lets you order your PEBES online, which the SSA then delivers via regular mail.

The key recommendations from the forums were:

- Interactive PEBES offers a valuable service that should be made available as widely as possible.
- Interactive PEBES must have additional disclosure and authentication safeguards to assure privacy.
- SSA needs to educate the public about its online disclosure and security protection to enable informed choice and ensure public confidence.
- SSA should consult continuously with private sector companies and other agencies to advance disclosure and security safeguards to assure the most up-to-date systems security procedures are in place.[83]

The issues clearly reinforced the desirability of PEBES Online, although changed from its original form. The actions following these panels included developing a new version of the system. The modified version will respond to the public's need for notice and choice. In addition, the SSA will make improvements in security and authentication. The recommendations of the forums have been incorporated into new features including:

- All personal PEBES information will be locked out of the Internet unless a member of the public requests his or her access to it. People who *opt-in* will be fully informed of the benefits and risks of unlocking PEBES Online. The PEBES Online statement will provide the requester with benefits estimates, the number of work credits earned, and whether the requester is insured for benefits. It will *not* provide his/her earnings history.
- Modified PEBES Online will be available only to people who have a registered e-mail account, such as one with an employer or with an Internet Service Provider. SSA will require requesters to use an activa-

How Modified Online PEBES Will Work

Internet user Jane Smith enters the Social Security Web site, Social Security Online (http://www.ssa.gov), to request unlocking of her personal Social Security record to receive a modified online PEBES. She completes an online form, including the following five pieces of personal information: name, Social Security number, date of birth, place of birth, and mother's maiden name. She also provides her e-mail address from her registered e-mail account. She reads a warning that, while the system meets appropriate security safeguards, no Internet system is 100 percent secure. Smith understands the benefits and risks, and she submits her PEBES request.

The next time she opens her e-mail, Smith finds a message from Social Security containing a plain-text, one-time "activation code." Smith must return to Social Security Online and again complete the online form, as well as submit the activation code to authenticate herself as the person to receive online PEBES. The next time she enters Social Security Online, she need only enter the five personal elements. She will receive her modified online PEBES. The statement will include estimates of her future retirement benefits and estimates of current survivor disability benefits payable. After receiving her estimates, Smith may re-lock her record if she wishes.

FIG. 10.5: How Modified Online PEBES Will Work

Source—Social Security Administration

tion code sent by SSA to their e-mail address. The code and the five pieces of personal authenticating information described earlier will unlock the modified online PEBES.[84]

The new system is indeed responsive to privacy control issues. As described in figure 10.5, you can now decide whether to opt-in to the system or not. You are not automatically part of PEBES Online. This gives you the choice and control of your information. Also, there will be *no* earnings information displayed. This feature responds to the extreme concern many Americans expressed when this sensitive information was combined with an Internet application. People are just not ready yet to have sensitive information, regardless of security precautions, on the Internet. The final change strengthens the security of the system by making sure no one but you can use PEBES Online to see your files.

The ability to order your PEBES statement on the Internet and have it delivered by mail continues to operate. This service, now called "PEBES by Mail," is available from 8:00 A.M. to 9:00 P.M. Monday through Friday, and 9:00 A.M. to 4:00 P.M. on Saturday (all Eastern Time). The interactive online system is still in development with no date set for its introduction. The SSA has identified and recruited privacy experts as advisors. While not an official committee, these experts with specialties in privacy, law, security, and finance will be available to consult regularly with SSA as it upgrades this service and offers new services in the future.

This case study points out the hazards even to the thoughtful and well-intentioned. The Internet offers efficiency and responsiveness in services. But when designing such services, developers of online systems must consider privacy concerns—not just system security. Incorporating privacy formally in design, test, and user education allows Web operators to reach you without misstep.

Government responsiveness, consumer action, and industry self-regulation all play a role in privacy protection on the Internet. What then is the role of the federal government? Is it sufficient that our executive branch encourage cooperation or should it take a more vigorous stance?

11

GOVERNMENT PRESSURE TO PROTECT YOUR PRIVACY

Privacy plays a role in every American's life. While some may require very little and others demand an excessive amount, it is a nerve that runs through us all. Our government recognizes this but finds the issue a conundrum. It must balance the competing values of personal privacy with the free flow of information. The latter is particularly significant because it is the fuel for the Internet and the Electronic Age. Yet, both values are important to a democratic society.

Wrestling with this balancing act, state legislators, the U.S. Congress, and our executive branch, including the Federal Trade Commission, are trying to adapt and spread policies of fair information practices. This chapter summarizes the actions to date of the varying governmental units and talks about the issues that are brewing but still lack clear resolution. The chapter concludes by moving across the Atlantic Ocean to Europe and explores the ramifications of the European Directive on Privacy Protection on U.S. businesses and on you.

FAIR INFORMATION PRACTICES

The National Information Infrastructure Task Force examined the issue of privacy on the information highway. In an option paper (www.iitf.nist.gov/ipc/privacy.html) released for public comment in April 1997, the Task Force outlines our national privacy heritage from a policy and legislative perspective. One area of agreement is the concept of fair information practices. Imbedded in these practices are the expectations every citizen should have. As a citizen, you should expect to have access to your personal information, to know that it is not improperly altered, and to be confident that it is relevant to the purported use.

You should also be prepared to make decisions about how you want your personal information used. Organizations, regardless of size or purpose, that collect personal information should disclose:

- Why they are collecting the information
- For what purposes they expect to use the information
- What steps will be taken to protect the confidentiality, quality, and integrity of the information collected
- Any rights of redress that are available to individuals for wrongful or inaccurate disclosure of their information

This list echoes at the national policy level the goals of the private sector's self-regulation efforts, the FTC agenda, and desires of citizens themselves. Privacy of personal information is an area in which all groups converge in principle. Other important issues remain in which viewpoints are not unified. Encryption, with its thorny issues of law enforcement access to all codes and the limitations of encryption export, is one example. In creating laws and regulations on both fair information practices and other privacy issues, the states are moving faster than the federal government.

WHAT THE STATES ARE DOING

The states may not be uniform in their approach to privacy, but they are active. Bills responding to concerns about the safety of children online;

spam; public records in areas of health, genetics, and related issues; and consumer privacy issues are all being debated in state assemblies and legislatures; and some of the bills are being enacted into law. In 1997, 133,212 bills were filed in the 50 states and the District of Columbia. Of these, 8,485 dealt with some aspect of privacy. This is a notable increase over 1993 when legislatures dealt with 6,629 privacy bills. By October 1997, 1,799 of the privacy bills had been enacted into law.[85]

The state front shows a lot of action; creative problem solving is going on at this level too. Legislation about unsolicited e-mail or spam has been stalled at state and federal levels. Proposed bills attack the problem by banning or limiting spam. The bills have met with opposition from unlikely comrades. The American Civil Liberties Union (ACLU) worries that such legislation limits freedom of speech. The Direct Marketing Association (DMA) is afraid it will set an untenable precedent for its members. Even though DMA members do not engage in activities even vaguely resembling spam, the wording of bills may overlap into the marketing arena in which they do participate.

California Assembly Bill 1629, which offers a new and different approach to the problem of spam, has been introduced into the California Legislature. It states that the ISP has the right to tell its users they cannot send spam. If the users fail to adhere to the ISP's policy, the ISP can prosecute. The issue is now framed differently. Instead of being about freedom of speech or limiting marketing activities, the legislation now states the hardware owner, the ISP, has the final say on what passes through its system. This is a simple and perhaps workable premise to use.

The activities going on in state legislatures on many privacy fronts provide models and examples of privacy standards and problem solving. But, they also provide an uneven patchwork of laws. When is it appropriate for Congress to legislate on privacy to guarantee certain basic rights?

THE RIGHT TIME FOR CONGRESS TO DECIDE

Our government—all parts of our government—traditionally react to crises. The Video Privacy Protection Act of 1988 is a good example of this. After Judge Robert Bork was nominated to the U.S. Supreme Court, a newspaper article detailing a number of personal facts about Judge Bork, including his questionable taste in videos, was published. His bad taste was proven by a list of movies he had rented from a local video store which the reporter had obtained. The reaction to this invasion of privacy was legislation protecting video records. This law protects just a corner of privacy and was pushed through based on a single, if shocking, event.

Another crisis of broader scope was the inappropriate activities of the credit bureaus that resulted in the Fair Credit Reporting Act (FCRA). While reacting to a hot issue, this legislation reached and helped many citizens. So did the laws protecting Americans from "Big Brother," the federal government. The most prominent is the Privacy Act of 1974, passed after the Watergate break-in. It limits federal collection of personal data to information that is "relevant and necessary" to accomplish the purpose of the agencies and hopefully some of government's misuse of personal information. This law was amended in 1988 with the Computer Matching and Privacy Protection Act. The Act regulates the use and exchange of information contained in existing agency databases. It is a clear recognition of the power of databases, especially when merged to develop more extensive information.

Later, Congress passed the Freedom of Information Act, which built on the Computer Matching and Privacy Protection Act, its predecessor. Not only did the government have to think carefully about what personal information it collected, but citizens had a right to access and see government records. Based on this legislation, people can write the FBI and ask for their files. These laws provide citizens with a form of disclosure and control in relation to the federal government.

Although, in part, reactions to crisis, these laws do provide Americans with thoughtful federal government privacy coverage. Is Congress ready to expand these guarantees to the private sector and the Internet? Probably not. Congress has been reluctant to address issues involving the Internet for a number of reasons. One is that the issues are often highly technical. Representatives and senators are not, for the most part, comfortable with the jargon and concepts of engineers or computer scientists. Most of them did not grow up with computers but were introduced to computer technology late. So there is some reticence. And related to this problem is the fact that technology changes swiftly. It is foolhardy to legislate based on the Internet of today because the advances will be great in 5 years and enormous in 10 years.

Rather than legislating on technology matters, Congress is preparing to start debate on a much more fundamental subject: the value of privacy to society in the electronic world. A robust discourse on principles could indeed lead to proactive and maybe visionary legislation, but it will take time and education to get there.

A first step was taken by Representative Rick White, Representative Rick Boucher, Senator Conrad Burns, and Senator Patrick Leahy when they formed the Internet Caucus. The founding caucus members urged their colleagues from both parties to learn about and to use the Internet. According to a letter the caucus posted to several Internet newsgroups, "From encryption to indecency, copyright protection to universal service, Congress will need to make prudent public policy decisions about a medium that presents such enormous opportunities for all Americans. Congress must not make these decisions without the full understanding of and familiarity with the Internet."[86]

To this end, the caucus has recruited over 100 members from the House of Representatives and the Senate. They have hosted forums on a number of Internet-related subjects. The forums bring in people and organizations from all sides of a topic. Gradually, these members of Congress are accumulating an understanding of the complex public policy issues. Understanding is an excellent basis for legislation.

THE MOST ACTIVE GROUP ON THE FEDERAL SCENE

Since 1995, the Federal Trade Commission has been privacy-active. It has stimulated debate, aired critical issues, and been a catalyst for action. In 1996 and 1997, the FTC held high-profile privacy workshops. People and organizations from all sides of the privacy issue spoke to the commissioners about their views. The messages heard during the workshops and the subsequent FTC actions covered:

- *Computerized Databases:* The "look-up" services were asked to speak to the widespread concerns raised by the collection, sale, and use of computerized databases with identifying information about consumers. During the 1997 workshop, these services offered the framework for a self-regulation initiative, which was developed and became formal in December of 1997.
- *Unsolicited Commercial E-mail:* One fact was crystal clear after the workshop panels dealt with this topic: Almost all consumers disliked unsolicited commercial e-mail. FTC staff is monitoring unsolicited commercial e-mail (spam) to see if it involves the fraudulent offering of products or services that could be unfair or deceptive. If fraud is proved, it is in violation of FTC regulations.
- *Consumer Online Privacy:* Consumers are concerned about their personal information in the online environment. The workshops developed industry interest in addressing this problem. FTC is working with the private sector and associations to educate consumers and increase confidence in the World Wide Web. Along with the educational activities, FTC will monitor Web sites to determine whether privacy practices are improving.
- *Children's Online Privacy:* The findings on this issue were disturbing. Children pose a unique problem when interacting on the Internet. Self-regulation by industry and technology can together provide effective tools to improve. The FTC will monitor Web sites to ensure improvement is occurring.[87]

The FTC has developed preliminary findings on a number of key privacy topics and begun a dialogue with those technologists and industry representatives who have solutions. This is significant progress for a short period of time. The issues, however, are difficult. Technology must be user-friendly or it will not be employed. Oversight and enforcement of self-regulation efforts is essential to make a difference. It is too early to tell whether either of these situations—user-friendly technology and self-regulation—will prevail. But it is a good time to reflect on progress to date.

At the request of Senator McCain from Arizona, the FTC in March and April scanned the World Wide Web and reported its findings to Congress on June 4, 1998. The scan checked to see if Web sites were gathering personal information and posting privacy statements explaining how the information would be used. They also looked to see if there was a way for you to opt out from supplying the information.

The general sampling methodology the FTC applied began with sampling size. They visited 1,401 Web sites. Of the sample, 212 were devoted to children's Web sites. The next 111 were non-children Web sites and were selected from the most popular sites on the Web. Another 404 focused on retail, health, and financial services. The remaining 674 Web sites were randomly chosen and aimed at consumer services. The FTC has had several "Surf Days" during the past three years where it has surfed the Web for consumer fraud or examined the practices on children's Web sites. This was an opportunity to compare progress over the past few years.

No significant improvement was reported. Some 85 percent of the sites collected personal information from consumers. Depending on the sample, as few as 13 percent disclose their information practices. The Commission's findings suggest greater incentives are needed for self-regulation and widespread implementation. The Commission will make its recommendations on this subject in the summer of 1998.

While no panacea has been discovered, the problem of privacy is being openly discussed and debated by all parties. Creating lasting solutions that will balance the democratic values of personal privacy with the free flow of information will take time. Ideally, the solutions will bring into existence the framework for Americans to interact with the Internet in a manner that permits the promise of commerce and reinforces privacy principles. But America may not have the time it needs to develop a thoughtful framework.

PROBLEMS FROM ACROSS THE OCEAN

The United States has a dispersed and decentralized privacy policy tradition, which includes reliance on voluntary commercial efforts. While we have several laws on privacy, such as FCRA, the Privacy Act, and the Freedom of Information Act, they were spawned in reaction to specific instances of abuse. No overarching law or regulation governing privacy exists. Also, no single person in the federal government is responsible for privacy. This lack of a single body of rules and a central leader for the privacy issue is at the heart of the problems the United States may face in October 1998.

The European Union (EU) is composed of 15 member countries: Belgium, France, Germany, Italy, Luxembourg, the Netherlands, the United Kingdom, Ireland, Denmark, Greece, Portugal, Spain, Austria, Finland, and Sweden. The EU has been exploring a European information policy for years in a very different way from the U.S. investigation. Given the vastly different cultures and governing systems, it is not surprising that its approach to information privacy has emphasized inclusiveness or dealing with all aspects of information privacy. Implementing broad policy was the European Union's objective; it has been working toward this goal for over a decade. The appeal of the topic began earlier, stemming in part from abuses and intrusions of personal information during World War II.

The United States has no comparable single broad privacy policy. The EU's policy has a centralized governmental focus and is highly regulatory, not voluntary, in its execution. You can find this policy, entitled "The European Council Directive on the Protection of Individuals with Regard to the Processing of Personal Data and on the Free Movement of Such Data," in full at www.privacy.org/pi/intl_orgs/ec/final_EU_Data_Protection.html. The policy contains 70 statements beginning with the word "Whereas." These "whereas" statements define the scope and intention of the EU.

The directive has two basic objectives:

- To protect individuals with respect to the "processing" of personal information
- To ensure the free movement of personal information within the EU through the coordination of national laws

To secure these two objectives, the EU has established a set of strict guidelines for the processing of personal information. One such guideline is on data quality, which is discussed in Article 6 of the directive. It states that all personal information must be processed fairly and lawfully. This way the person whose personal information is at issue knows it is being collected and used. The person must be informed of the proposed uses. Further, the uses cannot change. If a person provides information to obtain telephone service, that information cannot be used to target that person for information about vacation trips.[88]

Another guideline articulated in Article 25 is on the transfer of data outside the EU. This guideline is the most important one for the United States. It requires that member states enact laws prohibiting the transfer of personal data to nonmember countries that fail to ensure an "adequate level of [privacy] protection." When the protection is deemed inadequate, member states are required to take measures to prevent any transfer of data to the third country.

Does this guideline suggest the severe limiting of electronic information for global commerce? Maybe. Equally unclear are the repercussions for the United States. The questions our nation's leaders are sorting out include what constitutes "adequate level of protection," and do we meet this level? These questions are serious ones for us as citizens and U.S.–based businesses.

The issues are serious because of the amount of information that flows between the electronic borders of Europe and the United States. Multinational companies move information around the globe. It is not unusual for a company to maintain a centralized record-keeping and payroll in one location. This means the personnel files for the people working at the company's London office may be housed and run out of the company's Omaha, Nebraska, facility. If the United States does not meet the adequate information-protection level in the eyes of the EU, electronic transfer of paychecks for the London staff will be halted. And many other routine but vital systems of information flow would cease as well.

Credit card companies and insurance corporations operate on a global basis and require the transfer of information about individuals across borders to evaluate their creditworthiness or insurance risks. Citizens from any country can access the Web sites of companies based in other countries and purchase goods through the sites.[89] The EU directive can gravely disrupt the abilities of companies and the people who work for them to do business.

Resolving this problem has proven difficult. Two major problems have constrained the United States and the EU. The first problem is agreeing on what the term "adequate level of protection" really means. Then the United States and EU must determine if the U.S.'s policies and legal framework meet the definitions. We are handicapped in both of these endeavors by cultural differences. The United States would prefer a decentralized approach and leadership, in part, from our private sector. The private sector can move faster and be more flexible than a centralized government. The Europeans, on the other hand, depend on their governments for the vision of information privacy and the all-encompassing regulations necessary to make the vision a reality. These two approaches are so divergent that it is difficult to develop a middle ground satisfactory to both parties.

Each country in the EU has an independent public authority in charge of protecting personal data. This independent authority is often called a privacy minister. When the EU's privacy ministers talk to the United States, to whom do they talk? Do they speak to the White House's point man on the Global Information Infrastructure, Ira Magaziner; to Robert Pitofsky, chairman of the Federal Trade Commission; to William Daley, secretary of the Department of Commerce; or to any number of government officials involved in some part of the privacy debate? We have no single office or person responsible for privacy. Not having a comparable person at the matching level of government adds to the feeling of disappointment and annoyance already heightened by cultural gaps.

Both the United States and the EU are sincere in their desire to resolve these issues. Still, October may very well arrive without an acceptable definition of adequate privacy protection that the United States can meet. If this happens, do not expect a catastrophe. All electronic commerce over the Atlantic Ocean will not cease. American tourists will not be stranded in Europe with their credit cards rendered useless. It would not, however, be surprising to see the EU select U.S. industries or groups of companies that have practices unsatisfactory to the EU directive and insist on their reform.

The United States may be taking a different approach to privacy, but our government, companies, and citizens understand the importance of privacy principles. Many voices will be raised and many heard as consensus is developed for the public good. Action will follow consensus and will again be a joint effort. Innovative partnerships will form between the government and private sector, associations and nonprofits representing citizens from all over the country; and new laws and regulations will be the result.

The closing section is a resource guide for you. It lists general organizations monitoring the entire privacy arena and specific privacy groups like those focused on children or Internet fraud. Each is briefly reviewed along with an address of a Web site you can visit to learn more.

GUIDE TO PRIVACY RESOURCES

PRIVACY GROUPS AND RESOURCES

The Center for Democracy and Technology

A nonprofit, public interest organization working to create and advocate public policies that protect civil liberties and democratic values in computer and communication technology. The Web site contains headline articles regarding privacy, an example of the type of information companies can find out about you when you visit their Web sites, a link to The Anonymizer (allows you to surf the Internet anonymously), information on children's privacy, and a privacy page regarding health.

E-mail: Info@cdt.org
http://www.cdt.org
1634 Eye St., NW, Suite 1100
Washington, DC 20006
(202) 637-9800

Computer Professionals for Social Responsibility

A public interest alliance of computer scientists and others concerned about the impact of computer technology on society. The organization has a "Privacy and Civil Liberties" program and a Web page with information on its activities relating to privacy, privacy information, privacy resources, and other privacy links.

E-mail: cpsr@cpsr.org
http://www.cpsr.org
P.O. Box 717
Palo Alto, CA 94302
(650) 322-3778

The Electronic Frontier Foundation

A nonprofit organization working in the public interest to protect privacy, free expression, and democracy online. The site has headline news regarding privacy issues, a newsletter, and links to related sites.

E-mail: ask@eff.org
http://www.eff.org
1550 Bryant St., Suite 725
San Francisco, CA 94103-4832
(415) 436-9333

Electronic Privacy Information Center

This site has the latest headline news and privacy resources including a bookstore, previously classified government documents, an online guide to privacy legislation, practical privacy tools, and links to privacy resources.

E-mail: info@epic.org
http://www.epic.org
666 Pennsylvania Ave., Suite 301
Washington, DC 20003
(202) 544-9240

Privacy Rights Clearinghouse

A nonprofit consumer information and advocacy program that offers people the opportunity to learn how to protect their privacy. This Web page contains 20 fact sheets regarding privacy, resources to help cope with identity theft, speeches and papers regarding privacy, cases from the privacy hotline, and links to privacy resources.

E-mail: prc@privacyrights.org
http://www.privacyrights.org
1717 Kettner Ave., #105
San Diego, CA 92101
(619) 298-3396

Yahoo!'s Privacy Resources

Links to privacy resources, including links to indices of computer privacy, computer security and encryption, conferences, and software security sites.

http://www.yahoo.com/Law/privacy

INTERNATIONAL

Privacy International

Human rights group formed to be a watchdog on surveillance by governments and corporations. International privacy news, resources, and conferences can be found on this site. Also on this site are Web pages on ID cards, Mondex and Anonymous Digital Money, Outsourcing, Telephone Tapping and Encryption, and Video Surveillance.

E-mail: pi@privacy.org
http://www.privacy.org/pi
666 Pennsylvania Ave., SE, Suite 301
Washington, DC 20003
(202) 544-9240

Global Internet Liberty Campaign

An international coalition of nonprofit organizations addressing issues of free speech on the Internet, privacy, cryptography, and access. On this Web site: excerpts of the United States State Department Human Rights Guide, information on international privacy agreements, other privacy documents, and links to other related sites.

E-mail: info@gilc.org
http://www.gilc.org

TECHNOLOGY

Consumer Project on Technology

Information on privacy relating to medical records, other privacy-related documents, and links to other privacy organizations can be found on this site.

E-mail: love@cptech.org
http://www.essential.org/cpt/cpt.html
P.O. Box 19367
Washington, DC 20036
(202) 387-8030

The Codex

This Web site has a privacy page that provides many links to other privacy sites. It also educates laypeople on technology used in information gathering.

E-mail: SpyKing@thecodex
http://www.thecodex.com/index.html
2472 Broadway, Suite 328
New York, NY 10025
(917) 277-1983

Computer Security Resource Clearinghouse

National Institute of Standards and Technology
Department of Commerce
This site contains information on computer security specifically regarding crisis response, threats, vulnerabilities, and solutions.

http://csrc.ncsl.nist.gov

Cryptography, PGP, and Your Privacy

Web site that contains information on cryptography including FAQs and references, papers and books, cryptography utilities and services, and links to other cryptography sites.

E-mail: fran@world.std.com
http://world.std.com/~franl/crypto.html

Cypherpunks

This site has links to PGP, remailers, rants, various crypto-tools, news articles, and a mailing list.

http://www.csua.berkeley.edu /cypherpunks

Internet Privacy Coalition

The goal of this organization is to increase Internet privacy and security by increasing the availability of strong encryption and by decreasing export controls on cryptography. The Web page has headline news, upcoming events, information on the Golden Key campaign, pending legislation, resources, links to supporting organizations, and an IPC Alert for the latest news on crypto policy and the Golden Key campaign.

E-mail: ipc@privacy.org
http://www.privacy.org/ipc/

United States Department of Energy Computer Incident Advisory Capability

Computer security services for employees and contractors of the Department of Energy and links to reports on privacy issues can be found on this site.

E-mail: ciac@lllnl.gov
http://ciac.llnl.gov
(510) 422-8193

JUNKMAIL/SPAM

CAUCE (The Coalition Against Unsolicited Commercial E-mail)

A grassroots organization working to promote legislation outlawing UCE. Information regarding junk e-mail can be found on this site.

E-mail: comments@cauce.org
http://www.cauce.org

Unsolicited E-mail Resource Center

This site provides links to white papers, Web sites, blacklists, and newsgroups relating to spam.

E-mail: webmaster@seattlelab.com
http://www.seattlelab.com/slmail/uerc/links.htm

Scam Spam Reporting Page

This site is maintained by the Center for Democracy and Technology and the Voters Telecommunications Watch. It has a place to report incidents of junk e-mail scams and information on related lawsuits, legislation, and resources.

E-mail: webmaster@junkemail.org
http://www.junkemail.org/scamspam/

STALKING

Women Halting Online Abuse

The goal of this organization is to educate the Internet community about online harassment, empower victims of harassment, and develop policies to assist in the creation of harassment-free environments. The site has an online newsletter, a list of sites that have adopted and enforced anti-harassment policies, a list of "unsafe sites," resources, and information on what to do if you are harassed.

E-mail: whoa@femail.com
http://whoa.femail.com/

CONSUMERS AND BUSINESS

The Better Business Bureau

The site contains news releases relating to privacy and online forms to file complaints against businesses.

http://www.bbb.org
4200 Wilson Blvd, Suite 800
Arlington, VA 22203-1804
(703) 276-0100

The Direct Marketing Association

This site has information on protecting consumer's privacy, information for parents to help protect their children, and related privacy links.

E-mail: pr@the-dma.org
http://www.the-dma.org

FTC Bureau of Consumer Protection

This organization enforces a variety of federal antitrust and consumer protection laws. The site contains news releases, publications, and speeches; links to regional offices; formal actions, opinions, and activities; business guidance; economic issues; consumer protection; and antitrust/competition.

E-mail: consumerline@ftc.gov
http://www.ftc.gov
(202) 326-3128

National Consumers League Internet Fraud Watch

A nonprofit consumer organization that fights Internet fraud by improving prevention and enforcement. The Web page provides tips, articles, bulletins, and other information designed to help protect people against fraud and invasion of privacy.

http://www.fraud.org/internet
(800) 876-7060

CHILDREN

Center for Media Education

A nonprofit organization dedicated to improving the quality of electronic media for children and families. Relevant news articles, a campaign for children's television, and information on online advertising aimed at children can all be found on this Web site.

E-mail: cme@cme.org
http://www.cme.org/cme
1511 K St., NW, Suite 518
Washington, DC 20005
(202) 628-2620

Missing Kids/Child Pornography Tipline

A private, nonprofit organization that heads national efforts to locate and recover missing children. The organization also strives to raise public awareness about ways to prevent child abduction, molestation, and sexual exploitation.

http://www.missingkids.com
2101 Wilson Blvd., Suite 550
Arlington, VA 22201-3077
(800) 843-5678
(703) 235-3900

Children's Advertising Review Unit (CARU) Council of Better Business Bureaus

This Web site contains self-regulatory guidelines for children's advertising.

http://www.bbb.org/advertising/caruguid.html

Focus on Children

The home page contains news and articles from the "Internet Online Summit: Focus on Children" and links to Internet resources for parents.

webmaster@kidsonline.org
http://www.kidsonline.org

NetParents

The Web site was developed by a coalition of business, nonprofit, and public interest advocates and is a resource for parents. It contains information on children's blocking software, rating systems, and referrals to other Internet resources.

Webmaster@netparents.org
http://www.netparents.org

MEDICAL

American Health Information Management Association

Professional organization of health information management specialists that fosters the development of its members through education, certification, and lifelong learning, thereby promoting quality health information to benefit the public, the health care consumer, providers, and others users of clinical data.

E-mail: info@ahima.org
http://www.ahima.org
919 N. Michigan Ave., Suite 1400
Chicago, IL 60611
(312) 787-2672

National Committee on Vital and Health Statistics

This site contains the Department of Health and Human Services Subcommittee on Privacy and Confidentiality's hearings and meeting minutes.

http://aspe.os.dhhs.gov/ncvhs

GOVERNMENT POLICY

Department of Health and Human Services

This Web page includes Secretary Shalala's testimony and speeches on privacy and protection of health information and related reports.

http://www.hhs.gov

or

http://aspe.os.dhhs.gov/admnsimpo

National Information Infrastructure Task Force

An overview of privacy and other considerations as they relate to the National Information Infrastructure (NII) can be found at this Web page.

http://www.iitf.nist.gov/

PRIVACY JOURNALS

Privacy Journal
Box 28577
Providence, RI 02908
Monthly Publication
$118 per year ($145 overseas)
(401) 274-7861

Privacy Newsletter
Box 8206
Philadelphia, PA 19101
Monthly Publication
$99 per year ($149 abroad)
(215) 533-7373

Privacy Times
Box 21501
Washington, DC 20009
Bimonthly Publication
$225 introductory rate (may change this summer)
www.privacytimes.com
(202) 829-3660

Privacy and American Business
Two University Plaza, Suite 414
Hackensack, NJ 07061
Bimonthly Publication
$395 per year
(201) 996-1154

LIST OF ABBREVIATIONS AND ACRONYMS

AOL	America Online
BBB	Better Business Bureau
CARU	Children's Advertising Review Unit (part of BBB)
CME	Center for Media Education
DHHS	Department of Health and Human Services
DMA	Direct Marketing Association
EMR	Electronic Medical Record
EPIC	Electronic Privacy Information Center
EU	European Union
FBI	Federal Bureau of Investigation
FCC	Federal Communication Commission
FCRA	Fair Credit Reporting Act
FTC	Federal Trade Commission
GVU Center	Graphic, Visualization, and Usability Center at Georgia Institute of Technology
IFW	Internet Fraud Watch

IP	Internet Protocol
IPWG	Internet Privacy Working Group
ISA	Interactive Services Association
ISP	Internet Service Provider
IRS	Individual Reference Services
MLM	Multilevel Marketing
NCL	National Consumers League
NRC	National Research Council
NSA	National Security Agency
OSP	Online Service Provider
P3P	Platform for Privacy Preferences
PEBES	Personal Earnings and Benefit Estimate Statement
PGP	Pretty Good Privacy
PICS	Platform for Internet Content Selection
P-Trak/P-Find	Lexis-Nexis people locator products
SSA	Social Security Administration
SSL	Secure Socket Layer
SSN	Social Security Number
UCE	Unsolicited Commercial E-mail
W3C	World Wide Web Consortium
WWW	World Wide Web

GLOSSARY

BROWSER SOFTWARE

Software that is required on your computer to access, move between, and view written and graphical information on the Internet. Netscape Navigator and Microsoft Internet Explorer are examples of browser software.

BULLETIN BOARD

A public place on the Internet where people can post and read messages about specific topics or issues at their leisure. Bulletin boards often save messages for many months or years. Sometimes called newgroups, bulletin boards can be sponsored by any person or group. USENET and Deja News are examples of bulletin boards.

CHAT ROOM

A system that allows access by many people to send messages back and forth and see them on the computer screen. Chat rooms are the equivalent of a telephone conference call and can be sponsored by any person or group.

CLICK-STREAM DATA

Information gathered by some Web sites about where you move to and from on the Internet. Click-stream data collects information on the other Web sites you visit.

COOKIES

Bits of information that are sent from a Web site to your browser for storage. Cookies track your online activity at Web sites that use them for collecting information on the number of visits you make and your preferences when you visit the site.

CREDIT BUREAUS

Regulated companies that collect and manage the distribution of credit and financial information on individuals.

CYBERSPACE

A term that is used to refer to the digital world of online services and the Internet in general. Sometimes called the digital highway or information highway.

DOMAIN NAME

The "@" part of the Internet address or Uniform Resource Locator (URL) that identifies a specific Web site. The three character suffix assigned to U.S.–based Web sites normally identifies the type of organization, e.g., .com = company or business; .edu = educational institution; .gov = government agency; .org = nonprofit corporation. Some domain names have two character suffixes that identify the country where the Web site is located, e.g., .au = Australia; .uk = England.

ELECTRONIC MAIL

Also known as e-mail. Messages sent and received through the Internet or other online methods that can be read at the receiver's convenience. Your e-mail address is the unique name identifying you followed by the name of your Internet provider.

ENCRYPTION

Software used to code Internet and other online communications for security or privacy reasons. Encryption is used to protect credit card transaction information and other transactions that involve the transfer of funds or private information.

HOME PAGE

The first page of a Web site that typically introduces the Web site and its contents.

HYPERLINK

Also known as a link, this is a method for automatically moving within or between Web sites by pointing and clicking on text or an icon. Hyperlinks are shortcuts that eliminate the need to manually enter a URL every time you want to view a new page on the Internet.

ICON

Any graphic or picture on a computer screen that is used to start a software program, command the computer to perform a specific task, or move within or between Web sites. They are sometimes known as shortcuts.

INTERNET SERVICE PROVIDER (ISP)

A company which provides access to the Internet, usually for a fee, through its computer. The user normally gains access to the service by contacting the ISP through use of a modem.

PROFESSIONAL REFERENCE SERVICES

Companies that maintain databases on individuals and supply this information to businesses and government agencies.

PUBLIC-KEY INFRASTRUCTURE (PKI)

An agreed upon set of public and private enciphering keys that is the basis of the most widely used encryption methods used. Examples are PGP and RSA.

REALTIME

Communication between computers that occurs instantaneously. Chat rooms operate in a realtime mode.

SEARCH ENGINE

Software that searches the Internet for information. Users normally search for information using key words, phrases, or topics. Alta Vista and Lycos are examples of search engines.

SNIFFER

Software product used by hackers to obtain passwords and e-mail addresses without the users knowledge.

URL

Uniform Resource Locator identifies a location or page on the World Wide Web. URLs normally begin with http://www.

WEB PAGE or WEB SITE

Any document that can be viewed on the World Wide Web.

WORLD WIDE WEB

Also known as WWW, the part of the Internet that is generally available to the public.

REFERENCES

1. Ashley Dunn, "Tracking Crumbs of Data That Threaten to Define Us," *CyberTimes,* The *New York Times* on the Web, May 12, 1996, http://search.nytimes.com/books/search/bin/fastweb?getdoc+cyber-lib+cyber-lib+13789+10wAAA+.

2. Tom Forester and Perry Morrison, *Computer Ethics,* Second Edition, The MIT Press Cambridge, Massachusetts, 1994, 87.

3. Eugene Meyer, "Maryland Woman Caught in Wrong Net," *Washington Post,* December 15, 1997, C1.

4. Board of Governors of the Federal Reserve System, *Report to the Congress Concerning the Availability of Consumer Identifying Information and Financial Fraud,* March 1997, 5.

5. Federal Trade Commission, *Hearings on Privacy, Panel II: Who Uses Databases? What Are the Benefits and Risks?* Testimony by Beth Givens, June 10, 1997, 183.

6. Ibid., 184.

7. Ibid., 191.

8. Laurie J. Flynn, "Lexis-Nexis Flap Prompts Push for Privacy Rights," *CyberTimes,* The *New York Times* on the Web, October 13, 1996, http://search.nytimes.com/books/search/bin/fastweb?getdoc+cyber-lib+cyber-lib+7926+4+wAAA+.

9. Marc Rotenberg, "Lexis-Nexis Drops SSN Sales Plan," EPIC Alert 3.12, http://www.vortex.com/privacy/priv.05.14.z.

10. Carole Lane, "My View of Your Life; And Why Online Access Is Inevitable for Us All," *Washington Post,* July 13, 1997, C3.

11. Internet Services Association, "Protecting Your Privacy When You Go Online," http://www.isa.net/project-open/layout.html, 2.

12. Ibid., 4.

13. Robert H. Reid, *Architects of the Web, 1,000 Days That Built the Future of Business,* John Wiley & Sons, Inc., New York, 1997, 228.

14. "Surfer Beware: Personal Privacy and the Internet," http://www.epic.org/reports/surfer-beware.html, 1.

15. Ibid., 4.

16. Rebecca Quick, "Web Sites Start Using a Much Harder Sell," *Wall Street Journal,* April 24, 1997, B6.

17. "Junk E-mail," http://www.cauce.org/problem.html, 1.

18. George Johnson, "Junk E-Mail: From Trickle to Torrent," *Cyber-Times,* The *New York Times* on the Web, http://www.nytimes.com/library/cyber/week/052697junk.html, May 26, 1997.

19. Jared Sandberg, "AOL Declares Victory over Junk E-mail Firm," *Wall Street Journal,* December 19, 1997, B6.

20. "Bigfoot Files Multicount Suit Against CyberPromotions, Inc.," http://www.bigfoot.com/RUN?dyn=&FN=CYBERPROMO&locale=en&ver=1.0.0, New York, October 6, 1997.

21. Edward A. Robinson, "Beware—Job Seekers Have No Secrets," *Fortune,* December 29, 1997, 285.

22. Joan Indiana Rigdon, "Curbing Digital Dillydallying on the Job," *Wall Street Journal,* November 25, 1996, B1.

23. Ellen Alderman and Caroline Kennedy, *The Right to Privacy*, Alfred A. Knopf, New York, 1995, 313.

24. Ibid., 315.

25. Arthur Allen, "Exposed," *Washington Post Magazine,* February 8, 1998, 14.

26. "Should You Be Genetically Tested?" *Readers Digest,* January 1998, 180.

27. Bradley Graham, "Judge Blocks Navy's Discharge of Gay Sailor," *Washington Post,* January 27, 1998, A6.

28. Thomas Easton, "Let Your Modem Do the Walking," *Forbes,* November 17, 1997, 170.

29. Federal Trade Commission, *Fighting Consumer Fraud: The Challenge and the Campaign,* January 1997, 10.

30. Peter Wayner, "Bogus Web Sites Troll for Credit Card Numbers," *CyberTimes,* The *New York Times* on the Web, February 12, 1997, http://search,nytimes.com/search/daily/bin/fastweb?getdoc+cyber-lib-cyber-lib+5536+6+wAAA+.

31. "What Is Online Harassment?" Barton's Den of Iniquity, http://www.io.com/barton/harassl.html.

32. Matthew McAllester, "Live in Cyberspace/Ensnared in a Web of Harassment," http://www.geocities.com/~hitchcockc/newsday.htm.

33. Rebecca Quick, "On-Line Chat Can Be Safe—If You Know What to Say," *Wall Street Journal,* January 8, 1998, B5.

34. National Committee on Vital and Health Statistics, Department of Health and Human Services, *Testimony of Donald Palmisano Before the Subcommittee on Privacy and Confidentiality,* Hubert H. Humphrey Building, Room 4503A, 200 Independence Avenue, SW, WDC 20201, February 18, 1997.

35. National Committee on Vital and Health Statistics, Department of Health and Human Services, *Testimony of Steve Hoge before the*

Subcommittee on Privacy and Confidentiality, Hubert H. Humphrey Building, Room 4503A, 200 Independence Avenue, SW, WDC 20201, February 18, 1997.

36. Arthur Allen, "Exposed," *The Washington Post Magazine*, February 8, 1998, 28.

37. Janlori Goldman and Deirdre Mulligan, *Privacy and Health Information Systems: A Guide to Protecting Patient Confidentiality*, Center for Democracy and Technology, 1996, 9.

38. National Research Council, *For the Record Protection Electronic Health Information*, 1997, National Academy Press, Washington, D.C., 24.

39. National Committee on Vital and Health Statistics, Department of Health and Human Services, *Testimony of Neil Gallagher Before the Subcommittee on Privacy and Confidentiality*, Hubert H. Humphrey Building, Room 4503A, 200 Independence Avenue, SW, WDC 20201, February 18, 1997.

40. Congress, Senate, Senate Committee on Labor and Human Resources, *Testimony of Donna E. Shalala, Secretary of U.S. Department of Health and Human Services*, September 11, 1997, 2.

41. Ibid., 8.

42. Robert O'Harrow, Jr., "Prescription Sales, Privacy Fears," *Washington Post*, February 2, 1998, A1.

43. Center for Media Education, *Alcohol and Tobacco on the Web: New Threats to Youth*, WDC, March 1997, 11.

44. Federal Trade Commission, Hearings on Privacy, "*Children's Online Privacy, Panel 1B, Session Three: Parents' Perceptions and Attitudes on Online Information Collection from Children*," Testimony from Stanley B. Greenberg, Greenberg Research Inc., June 13, 1997.

45. Internet-Related Child Exploitation, Exploited Child Unit, "Enough Is Enough," http://www.missingkids.com/html/ncnec_defoutl_ec_internet_bckgrnd.htm, 1997.

46. "Reno to Convene Meeting on High-Tech Crime," *CyberTimes*, The *New York Times* on the Web, December 4, 1997, Associated Press,

http://search.nytimes.com/search/daily/bin/fastweb?getdoc+cyber-lib+cyber-lib+18265+0+wAAA+.

47. "From Porn to Cults: The Net Looks Nasty," *CyberTimes*, The *New York Times* on the Web, March 30, 1997, http://search.nytimes.com/search/daily/bin/fastweb?getdoc+cyber-lib+cyber-lib+11795+42+wAAA+.

48. Center for Media Education, "The Deceiving Web of Online Advertising," Fact Sheet.

49. Center for Media Education, "Update on Children's Web Sites' Information Collection Practices," http://tap.epn.org/cme/ftcrpt.html, 11.

50. Ibid.

51. Ibid.

52. Center for Media Education, *Alcohol and Tobacco on the Web New Threats to Youth*, WDC, March 1997, 29.

53. Ibid., 25.

54. Federal Trade Commission, Hearings on Privacy, *Panel V: Technology as a Tool for Addressing Children's Privacy Online, Testimony of Robin Raskin, Chief of Family, PC Magazine*, June 13, 1997, 16.

55. Federal Trade Commission, Hearings on Privacy, *Panel VI: Self-Regulatory Approaches, Testimony of Patricia Faley, Vice President of Consumer Affairs, The Direct Marketing Association*, June 13, 1997, 143.

56. Federal Trade Commission, Hearings on Privacy, *Panel V: Technology as a Tool for Addressing Children's Privacy Online, Testimony of Eric Wenger, New York State Attorney General's Office*, June 13, 1997, 46.

57. Federal Trade Commission, Hearings on Privacy, *Panel V: Technology as a Tool for Addressing Children's Privacy Online, Testimony of Jeffrey Fox, Assistant Editor, Consumer Union*, June 13, 1997, 30.

58. Rajiv Chandrasekaran, "Online Firms to Offer Own Curbs on Net," *Washington Post*, December 1, 1997, A1.

59. The Children's Advertising Review Unit, "1997 Self Regulatory Guidelines for Children's Advertising," http://www.bbb.org/advertising/caruguid.html, 8.

60. Deirdre Mulligan, Consultant, Center for Democracy and Technology, "Group of Experts on Information Security and Privacy, Workshop on Privacy Protection in Global Networked Society," "Privacy Protection in International Networks: A New Role for Technology," 1998, Organization for Economic Co-operation and Development, Room Document No. 4, February 1 and 17, 1998, 2.

61. Jonathan Wallace and Mark Mangan, *Sex, Laws, and Cyberspace,* Henry Holt and Company, Inc., New York, 1996, 42.

62. Bill Gates, *The Road Ahead,* Viking, New York, 1995, 107.

63. Ibid., 109.

64. Ibid., 110.

65. Ed Tiley, *Personal Computer Security*, IDG Books Worldwide, Forest City, California, 1996, 236.

66. Prepared Remarks of Christine A. Varney, Commissioner, Before the Privacy & American Business National Conference, Omni Shoreham Hotel, Washington, D.C., October 9, 1996, www.ftc.gov/speeches/varney/priv&ame.htm.

67. Federal Trade Commission, *Individual Reference Services: A Report to Congress,* December 1997, 14.

68. Robert O'Harrow, Jr., "Who's Got Your Number," *Washington Post,* March 10, 1998, A8.

69. Federal Trade Commission, *Individual Reference Services: A Report to Congress,* December 1997, 26.

70. Susan Fournier, Susan Dobscha, and David Glen Mick, "Preventing the Premature Death of Relationship Marketing," *Harvard Business Review,* January–February 1998, 43.

71. "No New Internet Taxes, For Now," edited version of President William Clinton's speech on February 26 to the Technology '98 Conference in San Francisco, *Washington Technology,* March 5, 1998, 6.

72. Federal Trade Commission, Hearings on Privacy, *Panel II: Self-Regulation Approaches to Online Privacy Issues, Testimony by H. Robert Wientzen, President and Chief Executive Officer of the Direct Marketing Association,* June 11, 1997, 87.

73. Ibid., 99.

74. Social Security Administration, *Privacy and Customer Service in the Electronic Age,* September 4, 1997, 35.

75. Ibid., 35.

76. Ibid., 37.

77. Simson L. Garfinkel, "Few Key Bits of Info Open Social Security Records," *USA Today Tech Report,* September 2, 1997, http://www.usatoday.com/life/cyber/tech/ctal94.htm, 2.

78. Social Security Administration, *Privacy and Customer Service in the Electronic Age,* September 4, 1997, 5.

79. Ibid., 6.

80. Ibid., 8.

81. Congress, Senate, Committee on Ways and Means, Subcommittee on Social Security, *Testimony of David C. Williams, Inspector General,* May 6, 1997, 2.

82. Simson L. Garfinkel, "Few Key Bits of Info Open Social Security Records," *USA Today Tech Report,* http://www.usatoday.com/life/cyber/tech/ctal94.htm, September 2, 1997, 1.

83. Social Security Administration, *Privacy and Customer Service in the Electronic Age,* September 4, 1997, 19–25.

84. Ibid., 30–31.

85. "The States and Consumer Privacy in 1997," Privacy and American Business Conference Report, Volume 4, Number 5, 1997/1998, 4.

86. http://www.house.gov/white/internet_caucus/letter.html. An open letter from the Congressional Internal Caucus to the Internet Community, March 28, 1996.

87. http://www.ftc.gov/os/9707/privac9b.htm

88. Barbara Wellbery, "An Overview of Information Privacy in the United States and European Union," *Privacy in Electronic Commerce: A Compendium of Essays on the Use of Information*, Edited by L. Richard Fischer, 1997, 72.

89. Ibid., 70.

INDEX

B

C

H

I

N

R

S

T

U

V

W

Y

Z

Also from Prima

Classes As Close As Your Computer!

Moving ahead in a career means updating your skills and education, but fitting traditional classroom study around hectic family and work schedules can be exhausting—plus the extra costs of commuting and child care really add up. The solution is online instruction, one of the hottest trends in higher education. From the comfort of your own home, you can hear lectures, participate in class discussions, and turn in assignments—all through the Internet. This comprehensive guide clearly explains how online education works, what equipment is needed, how to choose and apply to a school, and other vital information.

ISBN 0-7615-1370-1 / paperback / 216 pages
U.S. $16.00 / Can. $21.95

To order, call (800) 632-8676 or visit us online at www.primapublishing.com

To Order Books

Please send me the following items:

Quantity	Title	Unit Price	Total
______	How to Get a College Degree Via the Internet	$ 16.00	$ ______
______	______	$ ______	$ ______
______	______	$ ______	$ ______
______	______	$ ______	$ ______
______	______	$ ______	$ ______

*Shipping and Handling depend on Subtotal.

Subtotal	Shipping/Handling
$0.00–$14.99	$3.00
$15.00–$29.99	$4.00
$30.00–$49.99	$6.00
$50.00–$99.99	$10.00
$100.00–$199.99	$13.50
$200.00+	Call for Quote

Foreign and all Priority Request orders:
Call Order Entry department
for price quote at 916-632-4400

This chart represents the total retail price of books only (before applicable discounts are taken).

Subtotal	$ ______
Deduct 10% when ordering 3–5 books	$ ______
7.25% Sales Tax (CA only)	$ ______
8.25% Sales Tax (TN only)	$ ______
5% Sales Tax (MD and IN only)	$ ______
7% G.S.T. Tax (Canada only)	$ ______
Shipping and Handling*	$ ______
Total Order	$ ______

By Telephone: With MC, Visa, or American Express, call 800-632-8676 or 916-632-4400. Mon–Fri, 8:30–4:30.

WWW: http://www.primapublishing.com

By Internet E-mail: sales@primapub.com

By Mail: Just fill out the information below and send with your remittance to:

Prima Publishing
P.O. Box 1260BK
Rocklin, CA 95677

Name ______

Address ______

City ______ State ______ ZIP ______

MC/Visa/American Express# ______ Exp. ______

Check/money order enclosed for $ ______ Payable to Prima Publishing

Daytime telephone ______

Signature ______